Reality
in
Advertising

Reality
in
Advertising
by Rosser Reeves

N.W. Widener, Inc. 2015
  in association with
  Brand Team Six

Copyright © 1960, 1961 by Rosser Reeves

Originally Published April 17, 1961
By Alfred A Knopf, Inc. New York

First privately published by Ted Bates & Company, Inc.
In 1960 in somewhat shortened form

Reprinted over nineteen times

ISBNs: 978-0-9826941-3-8 (Hardcover)
        978-0-9826941-4-5 (Softcover)
        978-0-9826941-5-2 (Kindle)

Publisher's Cataloging-in-Publication Data
provided by Five Rainbows Services

Reeves, Rosser.
    Reality in advertising / Rosser Reeves.
        pages cm
    Originally published: New York : Knopf, c1961.
    ISBN: 978-0-9826941-3-8 (hardcover)
    ISBN: 978-0-9826941-4-5 (pbk.)
        1. Advertising. 2. Advertising—Management. 3. Branding
    (Marketing) 4. Marketing.   I. Title.
    HF5823 .R422 2015
    659.1—dc23

"After all, advertisements are purely functional things, and therefore the criterion is their success as advertisements and not as works of art. Commercial considerations are the judges, not a panel of any number of distinguished gentlemen."

H.R.H. the Duke of Edinburgh, to the jury who selected the Layton Annual Awards for Advertising, in London, 1960.

"Do you remember that in classical times when Cicero had finished speaking, the people said, 'How well he spoke'—but when Demosthenes had finished speaking, the people said, 'Let us march'?"

Adlai Stevenson, in introducing a candidate for the Presidency who succeeded where he failed, in Los Angeles, 1960.

Preface

This book attempts to formulate certain theories about advertising—many of them quite new, and all of them based on twenty years of the most intensive research.

Before the ink is dry, some man will sit down and write a campaign that ignores every word contained here. What is more, this campaign will work.

However, this does not invalidate this book. The croupier at a roulette wheel knows, too, that at some moment a player may violate all the rules of probability. If the wheel spins long enough, some number (say, thirteen) will come up twenty times in a row.

But roulette wheels, in the long run, do not lose money on exceptions, nor do advertising agencies or their clients, in the long run, make money on them. Agencies and clients, like actuaries, must invoke the laws of probability and determine (out of hundreds of campaigns) how they can make these laws work to their benefit.

As you will see, when the laws of probability are observed, it is possible to add a heavy percentage to every advertising dollar. Nor will this procedure rule out genius or fail to give genius full room to exercise its rich and golden talents.

I do not think it is out of order to say that it cost $1,000,000,000 to write this book. We spent that much of our clients' money, and made many mistakes, to isolate these principles.

Nor is it out of order to say that I alone did not write this book. It was written by a body of dedicated men and women who invested a fifth of a century, much of their profits, and a passionate curiosity to evolve a body of firm theory in a business where there is, to date, no really decent body of theory.

Like Mitya, in The Brothers Karamazov, *they wanted very much an answer to their questions.*

ROSSER REEVES

Contents

Reality
in
Advertising

1
A Common Fallacy

Madison Avenue is a street of myths and fables. One of the most popular of these is a notion, firmly rooted in many advertising men's heads, that a campaign can always be judged by its sales. Out of this comes one of advertising's oldest truisms:

"It's a good campaign, if sales go up."

The converse of this tired maxim, which is heard almost every day in agency circles, is:

"It's a bad campaign, if sales go down."

Unfortunately, neither of these statements is always true. They are very often false.

Winston Churchill, on the floor of the Mother of Parliaments, once observed: "There are two reasons for everything—a good reason, and the real one." This is particularly true in advertising; and before praising a campaign, or condemning it, it often pays to look for the real reason why sales may be going up or down.

Consider:

A famous razor-blade manufacturer had been running a brilliant campaign. Sales had been forging ahead. Then, by accident, millions of blades with defective steel were let loose on the market. Sales shot down, and the brand was almost crippled, but—the decline was not the fault of the advertising.

A great laxative had been running a strong campaign. For years it had produced a steady increase in sales. Then, an accident of chemistry made thousands of bottles highly toxic. The brand almost disappeared from the market, but again—the decline was not the fault of the advertising.

A food product, on the other hand, had been running a very poor campaign. Competitors were moving steadily ahead. Then, a change in product made the brand almost a household sensation, and sales shot up—with no change in advertising.

One of America's richest companies decided to enter the dentifrice field. Within a period of three years, this company introduced not one, but two major brands—spending over $50,000,000 in powerful advertising, sampling, and promotion. The share of market of many of the older brands, naturally, dipped down. It would be folly, however, to equate this decline with their advertising campaigns.

We do not mean to imply that advertising is not an enormous factor. It is. We simply wish to make the point that *big mistakes can be made* if you try to judge an advertising campaign, always, by sales.

Recently a group of marketing men, almost idly, at a luncheon table, listed thirty-seven different factors, any or all of which could cause the total sales of a brand to move up or down.

Advertising was only one of these.

The product may be wrong. Price may be at fault. Distribution may be poor. The sales force may not be adequate. Budget may be too low. A better product may be sweeping the market. A competitor may be outwitting you with strong deals. There are many variables.

And when a wheel has many spokes, who can say which spoke is supporting the wheel?

2
The Pulled and the Unpulled

"We've quips and quibbles heard in flocks, but none to beat this paradox!" sang Gilbert and Sullivan. So, you can't always judge a campaign by its sales? Then, all is lost, and the advertiser is cut adrift from reality!

Not necessarily.

Here, in fact, is the beginning of reality in advertising.

Follow us now in some very simple arithmetic. All you need, actually, is addition and subtraction, but we are going to use them in a new type of advertising research, one that throws a great white beam of light into many of the murky corners of advertising theory.

Conceive of the whole population of the United States divided into two huge rooms.

In one room, put all the people who do *not* know your current advertising. They do not remember what it said; they do not recall having seen it, read it, or heard it; their minds, as far as your advertising is concerned, are complete blanks. Now, walk into this room and interview these people. Find out how many are using your product.

Let us say that 5 out of every 100 people who do not know your advertising (or 5%) are customers.

Since these five people do not know your advertising, it is obvious that they must have chosen your product in another way. Perhaps a friend told them about it. Perhaps you gave them a free sample. Perhaps their doctor recommended it. Perhaps they were led to it by an old campaign that they have now forgotten. Perhaps they learned about it, as children, from their mothers and fathers. But they did not become customers as a result of your current advertising, because they do not know your current advertising.

Now, walk into the other room. Here are the people who *do* remember your advertising. They can prove that they know it, because they can tell you, correctly, what it says.

Let us say that 25 out of every 100 people who do know your advertising (or 25%) are customers.

From 5% to 25%! Now you have one of the most exciting statistics in modern advertising. For it tells you that if you ran no advertising at all, for a while you would sell 5% of the people, but that *out of every 100 people who remember your advertising, an extra 20 are being pulled over to the usage of your product.*

The pulled vs. the unpulled!

Now total sales may be going up and down, due to many other reasons, but where your copy has registered, you know that you are getting an extra 20%—pulled over by copy, and by copy alone.

The figure may be 20, 18, 14, 10, 6, or 3. Worse yet, it may be zero. Worse even than zero, it may be minus 3, or minus 10.

For as you will see, the people who read and remember your advertising may buy less of your product than people who are not aware of your advertising at all. Your advertising, in other words, may, literally, be driving away customers.

Now, for the first time, you have a way to measure a campaign—without reference to the many other variables. You can look through the variables and see just what you are getting for your advertising dollars.

3
Inside 180,000,000 Heads

Franklin Delano Roosevelt was questioning a physicist from Los Alamos, who kept insisting that a certain thing could not be done.

"But you keep saying it is *theoretically possible*," persisted Roosevelt.

"Yes," said the physicist. "It is also theoretically possible to count every grain of sand in the Sahara desert. But practically, it cannot be done."

To laymen who do not understand research, it may seem equally impossible to divide the whole population of the United States into two huge rooms. But, as research professionals know, all that is needed is a broad enough sample—one wide enough and deep enough to reflect the total population.

Such a sample is difficult, it is expensive. We have made many mistakes in working out the details, but we break down the whole population into the people who remember the big package-goods campaigns and those who do not; and we then measure the number of people in each group who are actually using the advertised product.

Such research will startle any advertising man who undertakes it. What rich, rich rewards! For the first time, you get a fascinating look into 180,000,000 consumer heads —which campaigns people remember, and which campaigns cause them to buy. *It shows us, too, as you will see, an astonishing number of campaigns that people don't bother much to remember,*

as well as a large number of campaigns that do not
cause any of the people to buy.

At regular intervals we interview thousands of
people in 275 different locations from coast to coast.
The sample is carefully broken down into age, income,
race, and city size. We measure only big advertising
campaigns. The largest appropriation is $17,500,000.
The smallest is $400,000. The average budget for each
brand is approximately $5,000,000 a year.

We measure:

1. *The number of people who remember (and who
do not remember) your current advertising. We
call this* PENETRATION.

2. *The number of customers in each group. The
difference in these two figures shows how many
have been pulled over to the usage of your product
by your advertising. We call this* USAGE PULL.

Such a study for one brand, in one year, would take
much of the guesswork out of an advertising program,
for as the ancient proverb reads: "In the country of the
blind, the one-eyed man is king."

However, a single study is very much like a single
observation of the stars when a racing sailboat is at
sea. It may tell you exactly where you are at that precise
moment, but it will not reveal where you have been,
how fast you are moving, nor how to judge the winds
and currents which are carrying you along.

Nor does it tell you the speed, position, and course
of your competitors.

But when such a study is made for hundreds of brands—when the results are compared, year after year, and the campaigns behind the changes are analyzed to find out basic causes—the findings are of immense value.

Now the advertising race becomes startlingly clear. We know the speed, position, and course of all the boats. We know where we are, where we are going, and when to change direction. Now there are charts to guide us, buoys to mark the reefs, and lighthouses to indicate safe harbors.

A famous company president once said:

"Advertising, to me, is really one of the mysteries of American business. I can inventory my stock. I can calculate the cost of my factories. I can figure my taxes, estimate my depreciation, determine my sales cost, derive my return per share. Yet, there are times when I spend as much as $18,000,000 a year on advertising— and have no idea what I am really getting for my money."

He is not alone. Advertising, far too often, is a mysterious vortex into which millions of dollars are poured every year. These dollars swirl down and around and are sucked out of sight; and at the end of the year, company officials are often left to guess just what it was they bought with these heavy disbursements.

One of the world's largest manufacturers put it another way. He said:

"I know that at least half of my advertising money is being wasted. My problem is—I do not know which half."

Our studies of penetration and usage pull begin to answer this problem.

For the first time, we have an auditing approach to advertising.

For the first time, we can begin to peer through advertising's seventh veil.

And to say that we have uncovered some startling advertising truths is to put it very mildly.

4
The Penetrated People

Here is the first half of one of these studies. It is just seventy-eight black bars on a much-simplified chart; but no advertising man will ever want to forget it, for it is a chart pregnant with immense implications.

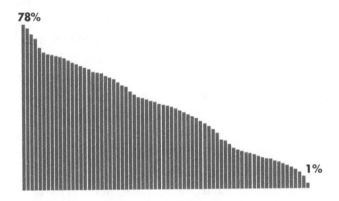

Each one of these bars shows the percentage of the population penetrated by a famous advertising campaign. You will see that one advertiser has successfully put his message into 78% of the heads; another, into only 1%. We have not bothered to put down the percentages over each bar; but, as you can see, there are some startling disparities. Some of these advertisers have penetrated 50%, 60%, 70% of the entire population—and some, only 4%, 5%, and 6%.

Just a chart with seventy-eight black bars?

No. Here, indeed, is the beginning of reality in advertising—a picture, in cold black and white, of the accomplishments of seventy-eight of the biggest package-goods advertisers in the United States. In the past twenty years, these companies have spent billions of dollars to buy this penetration. Scores of agencies, thousands of brilliant men, have labored to register these advertising campaigns with America's 180,000,000 people. Soaps and cigarettes, cake mixes and candies, cereals and soft drinks, frozen pies and shave creams, laxatives and beers, toothpastes and margarines and fruit juices—here they all are, and others, too.

It is the first time in the history of advertising that a measurement of this size and scope has ever been made. Publication of the brand names would cause a wave of protest and denunciation, for many proud companies would be shocked to see how little they have received for years of huge expenditures.

However, the real truths are not so much in the bars. They lurk behind the bars. We must sift them out of the data, as we compare one brand with another brand, and measure the money each has spent to achieve these results.

Then, our eyebrows begin to rise.

The shape of reality in advertising begins to appear.

Some of advertising's most lofty clichés begin to appear as just that—clichés, or old wives' tales, utterly divorced from reality.

Out of hundreds of accumulated case histories, which would call for many books far thicker than this, let us give you, by way of introduction, just four examples:

Case History No. 1
On this chart is an advertiser who is spending
$2,000,000 a year. He has put his message into
the heads of only 5% of the people.

Yet his biggest competitor—and this is almost
certainly why he is the biggest—has in less time
and with less money registered his story with
over 60% of the people, i.e., has put his message
into 1,200% more heads with a smaller number
of dollars.

Case History No. 2
Hidden in this chart are two advertisers, each
spending $10,000,000 a year, who changed their
stories at the same time.

One year later, one of these had registered
his new message with 44% of all the people in
America.

The other, despite the same amount of money,
had managed to get his message into only 1.8%
of the heads.

Here is a difference of 2,200% in penetration,
with equal budgets. The errors committed blindly
by the second advertiser resulted in the virtual
death of his brand.

Case History No. 3
One of these bars represents a food advertiser
who has a very strong story. Yet, this advertiser
is using a dramatic device in his campaign
that overrides his story and is washing out
his copy line.

Only 9% of the people remember his copy, and 38% of the people are remembering a useless device which contains no message.

Case History No. 4
Here is an advertiser who once had one of the highest penetrations in the United States. He did not change his story, but he changed the way he told it.

He has dropped half of the penetration that cost him millions to accumulate; yet, he is unaware of it, for he does not have a measurement of this kind.

Advertising history flows up and down a procession of bars like these. Some day a separate book will be written, when all the figures can be released; for when the ebb and flow of these charts are analyzed, year after year, and when the campaigns behind the charts are analyzed to find out what caused the changes, many things are made clear for the first time.

What types of advertisement deliver the message best? What happens when a company changes its message too often? When does an advertising campaign wear out? How much of a campaign can the consumer usually remember? What is the life expectancy of a campaign? What are some common, and unrevealed, mistakes that can cripple a campaign? How can you lower the penetration of your competitors? What ways are there to deliver a given message at a lower cost? How effective is brand-image advertising? Will you deliver the message better by advertising to

5,000,000 people, say, twenty times—or by reaching 50,000,000 twice? All these subjects, and a good many others, will be covered in this book.

Penetration,[1] however, is concerned only with sinking the message home. Even more important is: "What message do you wish to sink home?"

[1] In this book, for purposes of simplicity, penetration is described as a perfect research tool. Of course, it is not. There are important statistical considerations, such as feedback and correlation. In all of the case histories in this text, however, the statistical difference is of such a magnitude that these factors can be ignored.

5
The Pulled-over People

We have all heard the story of the man who walked into a small country store and found it stacked from floor to ceiling with hundreds of bags of salt.

"I see you sell salt," he said to the storekeeper.

"No," said the storekeeper, "I don't sell salt."

Then he added, rather wistfully: "But could that salesman sell salt!"

What we have read so far about penetration does not tell whether or not our salesman can sell. We can have a large body of penetrated people and get no sales.

A man may shout from a housetop. He may blow a golden whistle and sing and dance. Because of his strange antics, people may remember what he says; but what he says may not lead them to buy.

A company with a strong message may get its story into the heads of only a few people, and become rich. Conversely, a company with a bad message may get its story into all the heads, and become bankrupt.

Usage pull measures this difference. It is not concerned with the amount of penetration. Instead, it asks only one question:

Does your story work?
Does it pull people over to your product?

When we redraw our previous chart in this new light, and change the bars according to whether these seventy-eight advertising campaigns are strong or weak, we see a most astonishing difference. Again, we have a chart with immense implications:

Here the horizontal line represents the average number of people pulled over by the copy in a given product classification. The companies above the line have stronger stories, which are producing more customers. The companies below the line have weaker stories—many of them, in fact, so weak that they are producing no new customers at all.

Here again, if we were to reveal the brand names, is a chart that would cause emergency meetings in boardrooms from coast to coast. For here, in simple numbers, is revealed the almost incredible difference in the purchasing power of advertising dollars in the hands of different advertisers.

Again, the lessons are legion:

19 /

Case History No. 1
Two years ago an advertiser had a great story.
Out of every 100 people who remembered it,
20% were pulled over to his product. Then, he
changed his campaign.
Today, he is running a story which pulls over
only 10%. His advertising message is only one
half as effective—yet he is not aware of it, since
he lacks a measurement of this kind.

Case History No. 2
An advertiser spending $4,000,000 a year has
a story with enormous usage pull. It actually
pulls over 18% of the people who register it in
their brains. Yet his story is hidden in a small
box in his advertising.
What he is saying, meanwhile, in his head-
lines and pictures is doing him no good.
What copy surgery he could perform, if only
he knew these facts!

Case History No. 3
In this chart is an advertiser spending $7,000,000
a year.
Yet, his campaign has no usage pull!
This is extraordinary. One would assume
that at least the advertising is getting the brand
name before the public—and that this would
sway some of the public.
Not so.
When we check the people who do not remem-
ber the advertising, we find they use just as

much of the product as the people who do remember the advertising. What a tremendous waste of advertising dollars!

Case History No. 4
Indeed, the picture may be even worse.
In this chart is a great beer manufacturer, spending over $10,000,000 a year. In his advertising, he uses one dominant, memorable picture theme. Millions of people remember this picture theme, but it repels them. Those who remember this picture theme actually drink less of his beer.
It would be worth millions of dollars to this man to make one simple change.

It will pay you to read, and reread, these four case histories. We have cut them to the bone, so that each is summed up in only a few dozen words; but it is not impossible that you may be making these same mistakes in the advertising campaign that you are writing now, or running today, or planning to run tomorrow. For these are not isolated case histories; they are just four out of hundreds which are being re-enacted, year after year, by many sophisticated advertisers.

You may have switched to a story that is only one-half as effective, without knowing it.

You may be concealing your most potent copy, hiding it behind some dramatic device which is actually doing you no good.

You may be running a story which is bringing you no new customers—in other words, running a quite useless campaign.

Or, even worse, you may be running a campaign which is actually driving away customers—a campaign which, where it registers with the consumer, is actually depressing your sales.

Now the picture of reality in advertising becomes even clearer, and we begin to see the inner workings of some campaigns, which are almost household words.

We see that people everywhere can be talking about a sensational new campaign; the client can be happy; and the agency filled with pride. Yet, the campaign may be no more than a beautiful but empty gesture. In fact, it may even be driving away customers.

We see that to the penetrated people, we must add the pulled-over people.

Some of America's most admired campaigns suddenly appear as hollow shells—beautiful, perhaps, to look at, but empty of sales content and purpose. Other campaigns, hardly noticed by the profession, are suddenly seen to be brilliant *tours de force* of persuasion and salesmanship.

6
The Extra Edge

"Let me taste the dish," said Brillat-Savarin, "and you can spare yourself the rhetoric on how well you cook."

This is by way of saying that the previous pages may sound enormously persuasive. Here is a new type of research, done on a scale never before seen in the advertising business, and it throws forth some facts which would give any advertising man pause. But the only purpose, of course, is to get better advertising; and it is proper at this time for the reader to ask some blunt questions:

"When you have summed up all these principles which you are now beginning to develop, do they really show advertising in a new light? Do they result in more effective advertising? Will they give a company an extra edge?"

The answer to all these questions is "Yes." Many new principles of advertising begin to crystallize, and they do, indeed, give a company an extra edge.

This book cannot set forth, in detail, a fifth of a century of massed data. However, beneath the statistics, the laws of cause and effect can be seen at work. Like a millstone, they grind slowly, but they grind exceedingly fine. Patterns begin to emerge; the patterns shape themselves into principles; the principles, tested and retested by further observation, begin to appear as laws of reality in advertising.

There are, of course, no certainties. George Meredith said all that was to be said on this subject when he wrote: "Ah, what a dusty answer gets the soul, when hot for certainties in this our life." However, studies of companies which have applied these principles show that they achieve a penetration 15.4% higher than the average of competing brands, and a usage pull 16.2% higher.

When we combine these figures (and it is not as simple as adding them together)[1] we find that they represent an increase in campaign effectiveness of 34%. *This means that these campaigns are working 34% harder than the average of some of the most sophisticated campaigns in America.*

A $3,000,000 budget, in essence, becomes $4,000,000.

To a company that is not achieving this extra edge, the difference is not so much money lost as it is sales lost. For a sale is regenerative; it is a chain reaction that spawns profits year after year as the customer returns again and again, to buy more and more.

The lost sale, genetically, is like the baby that was never born.

Keep in mind, too, that we are measuring only big advertisers, with big brands. These companies command the top advertising talent, they spend the most money, and they live or die by advertising. We are measuring the giants.

If we were to calculate this percentage against a much more general level of advertising, we believe that the extra edge would be much higher.

[1] Statistically, the penetration has an index of 115.4, or 1.154 times average penetration. The usage pull has an index of 116.2, or 1.162 times average usage pull. And 1.154 × 1.162 = 1.341, or 34%.

7
The Life Expectancy of Advertising

The Red Queen, in *Through the Looking Glass*, was an exceedingly ill-tempered person, but perhaps she had a reason to be: she had to run at top speed to stay in the same place.

Every advertiser, whether he knows it or not, is very much like the Red Queen—for he, too, is doomed, as long as he advertises, to run at top speed in an effort to stay just where he was months, or even years, ago.

Many advertisers, in fact, are in even worse shape. For as we have seen from some of our penetration case histories, some advertisers may not stay in the same place even when they *do* run at top speed. The public has an appallingly ephemeral memory; penetration, bought and paid for with millions and millions of dollars, can drift away like morning fog; and a good many of the realities of advertising stem from this fact.

As Arthur Nielsen puts it: "We spend our lives trying to fill a leaking bucket."

Let me tell a story:

A few years ago, we performed an experiment to determine the life expectancy of penetration. How long does a person remember a campaign, once he has it in his head? When does some other advertising crowd it out?

We found out the exact number of people who remembered the advertising of a big brand which we handle.

50% knew it, and 50% did not. We kept the names and addresses of these people (something not normally done as a matter of course), and six months later went back to the same people.

Keep in mind that the same campaign was still running.

We were astonished to discover that half of the people who had known our story had now forgotten it; and half of those who had not known it could now describe it.

If you want a picture of "The Passing Parade," in very simple but very depressing form, here it is:

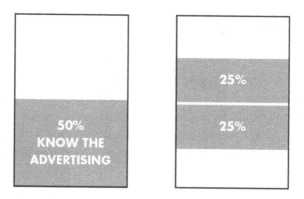

You will see, from the bar on the left, that 50% of the people knew our story when this survey was made. But now glance at the bar on the right. Six months later, 50% still know the story—but half of the old group has forgotten it, and a new group has taken their place.

Again, we must caution you that this is not an isolated experiment. It is not true of just one brand. It is true of all brands; and what is more, there is an important corollary:

The advertiser given in the example above managed to maintain the same penetration by continuing the same story and by continuing the same pressure of advertising dollars. Had he changed his story, or lowered the pressure of his advertising dollars, he would have witnessed a sudden and very painful drop—for either one, or both, of these reasons.

Recently we watched the drama of an advertiser who had 65% penetration on a powerful, sales-winning theme. Then he changed campaigns. In eighteen months, his hard-won 65% penetration had dropped to 2.2%—in other words, had almost vanished entirely.

As you will see later, this constant shifting of penetration has enormous implications in the reality of advertising. It is going to force us to do a good many things we might not otherwise do. We must keep in mind that $43,000,000,000 a year is being spent for penetration. This is the rather staggering sum of $117,000,000 a day, spent in a desperate attempt to buy brands a bit of space in the memory box of the consumer. He is a beleaguered consumer, a confused consumer, battered by television, assailed by print, assaulted by radio, bewildered by posters. It is very difficult to get him to remember, and he is very prone, indeed, to forget.

Penetration is volatile.

Like vapor, it can melt into thin air.

Like the mercury in a barometer, penetration is supported by pressure—the pressure of the same story, and of advertising dollars. When the pressure falls, or the story changes, the penetration barometer falls; and your chance to exercise your usage pull comes down just as fast.

8
The Multi-Million Dollar Error

There are two fables in the mythology of ancient Greece which every advertising man would do well to remember. One is the story of Tantalus, immersed in clear fresh water up to his neck, and dying of thirst; for every time he stooped to drink, the water receded from his lips. The other is the story of Sisyphus, doomed to roll a huge stone to the top of a mountain; yet each time he neared the top, the stone would roll down to the bottom again.

These stories are re-enacted every day in the advertising business. Yet, there is an abundance of clear, fresh water, and there are easy ways to drink it; and there are simple engineering principles that can easily move the stone to the top of the mountain.

It is difficult, out of hundreds of lessons taught by penetration and usage pull, to pick just a few for a book as slim as this. However, one of the biggest is this:

Too-frequent change of your advertising campaign destroys penetration.

Here, indeed, is the "Multi-Million Dollar Error." It is one of the oldest principles in advertising, yet none is more generally ignored; for there are few brands on the market today that have not changed campaigns 5, 10, 15 or 20 times in the past 20 years.

"This story is worn out," a manufacturer will say.

"The public is getting bored with it," another will tell you.

"A new story puts new pep into my brand profile," a third will confide.

If 90% do not remember it, the story is certainly not worn out. If 90% are not even aware of it, they can hardly be bored. And as for the new-pep philosopher, if only he had the figures, he would discover that by changing his story he is simply getting his brand profile into as few heads as possible.

If an advertiser spends $2,000,000 a year, and does not change his basic appeal, and if he creatively utilizes other principles which will be set down later in this book, he will find that it is possible to register his story with roughly 40% of the people.

If the advertiser is really expert, he can do much better. We have one brand, spending $2,500,000 a year, which has a penetration of 70%. This means that seven out of every ten people in America know the advertising.

However, there are advertisers spending over $10,000,000 a year who, through change, have kept their penetration as low as 15%.

Let us examine this common error of too-frequent change, in detail, in terms of a package-goods company.

A Case History
The president of a company has been spending $5,000,000 a year for five years. Each year, a fresh burst of discontent (some call it "genius") has dictated a new campaign. In this time, his company has run five different campaigns.

A study of penetration case histories over a long period of time leads us to believe that,

*with a single, uninterrupted campaign theme,
he might now have achieved a penetration of at
least 60%. This means that six out of every ten
people in America would now know his story.
Instead, we find him with a penetration of 15%.
He has settled for 75% less advertising power. He
has paid $25,000,000 for penetration which he
might have bought for about $6,250,000.*

Such men, actually, are engaged in the business of
cutting down their own trees. Some of these trees are
hacked down as mere saplings. Some are chopped down
just as they begin to grow straight and strong and tall.
And sometimes we witness one of the most senseless
things in the advertising business: a new management
brings crashing to earth one of the giants of the forest,
apparently for no other reason than a desire to rear-
range the advertising landscape.

At this point we hear a quiet voice asking: "Yes, but
when a campaign gets very high penetration, when
almost everybody in the country knows it, does it not
then begin to wear itself out?"

The answer, of course, is still "No." Penetration statistics prove this. For if the campaign wore itself out, one
of two things would happen: penetration would drop,
or the public would cease to respond to the message,
and usage pull would fall.

We have never seen such a thing happen, unless
the product suddenly becomes outmoded. Instead,
the campaign continues to flourish, like a great tree
spreading its branches and reaching for the sun. And

year after year, rich and fruitful seeds continue to sift down to the earth, in new sales and customers.

A famous dental cream campaign has been running for twenty-two years and has kept this brand in first place in spite of massive onslaughts from its competitors. A famous bread campaign has been running for sixteen years, and the branches continue to proliferate. A great mouthwash campaign ran for thirty-three years. A cigarette campaign has been running for twenty-one years. Another cigarette campaign ran for eleven years. A campaign for a deodorant soap ran for over twenty-five years. A candy campaign, with a relatively small budget, has been running for seven years and has one of the highest penetrations in the United States. A great headache remedy ran the same campaign unchanged for over twenty years. One drug company, now a giant corporation, founded its business on a single product—and ran the copy unchanged for thirty-one years.

There are many examples.

Three great basic principles of advertising reality emerge from our research:

1. *Changing a story has the same effect as stopping the money, as far as penetration is concerned.*

2. *Thus, if you run a brilliant campaign every year, but change it every year, your competitor can pass you with a campaign that is less than brilliant—providing he does not change his copy.*

3. *Unless a product becomes outmoded, a great campaign will not wear itself out.*

So let your tree reach for the sun! In fact, clear away the advertising underbrush, and give it a chance to grow and breathe. You can own a towering giant, with its roots deep in the earth, safe against even the most raging advertising storms.

9
The Advertising Burning Glass

A story goes that old Calvin Coolidge, sitting patiently in a stern little New England church, listened attentively to a minister who had preached steadily for two hours. A friend, later, asked him what the sermon was about.

"Sin," said Coolidge.

"What did he say?" persisted the friend.

"He was against it," said Coolidge.

The story has a value to advertising men, for it illustrates a reality principle made crystal clear by a study of hundreds of penetration case histories. The principle is this:

The consumer tends to remember just one thing from an advertisement—one strong claim, or one strong concept.

The advertisement may have said five, ten, or fifteen things, but the consumer will tend to pick out just one, or else, in a fumbling, confused way, he tries to fuse them together into a concept of his own.

Reality campaigns, those that climb the ladder of penetration with the most speed, do not put the consumer in this predicament. Instead, they gather their energies together into a tight coil. They present him with one moving claim or concept which he can easily remember. Like a burning glass, which focuses the rays of the sun into one hot, bright circle, they bring together all the component parts into a single incandescence of their own.

We do not mean that the campaign should not say a dozen things about the product. These can add depth, color, dimension, and persuasiveness. In fact, they are very often the difference between "telling" and "selling."

A legendary copywriter, reading a galley of this book, put it another way: "I like to think of the bits and pieces of a product's individuality as pieces of tile. They must be assembled, like a mosaic, into one striking and memorable theme, for the public simply cannot carry all the individual pieces in its head."

A President of the United States, while running for office, covered fourteen different points in one of his speeches. It was a clear and vigorous speech. Despite its clearness, however, a study made the next day showed that less than 2% of the people knew what he had said. Had he picked one point of focus, he might have had 30%, 40%, or 50% remember the substance of his message.

Marcus Cato, the Roman orator, understood this principle perfectly when he focused a whole series of speeches into the thunderous phrase: "Carthage must be destroyed!" With it, he put an end not only to a city but to a civilization.

Long after Americans had forgotten Franklin Delano Roosevelt's first inaugural address, they remembered, in essence, all that there was, when they remembered: "The only thing we have to fear is fear itself!"

William Jennings Bryan knew this perfectly: "You shall not press down upon the brow of labor this crown of thorns! You shall not crucify mankind upon a cross of gold!"

Winston Churchill practiced it instinctively: "Never... was so much owed by so many to so few!"

An advertising theoretician who read the above paragraphs entered a demurrer. "I don't know about that," he said. "I might write an advertisement and list twenty-five separate advantages, and it might cause the consumer to rush right out and buy."

This is true.

However, we are discussing penetration—which may be defined as "what it is possible for the consumer to carry in his head." For most people do not rush right out and buy.

The same advertising man, when asked to name some of the great advertising campaigns, rattled off: "HALITOSIS" ... "LIFEBUOY AND B.O." ... "L.S.M.F.T. AND THE CHANT OF THE TOBACCO AUCTIONEER" ... "IT'S TOASTED" ... "WHICH TWIN HAS THE TONI?" ... "THOSE THREE STREAMS OF BUBBLES WHICH PROVE ANACIN BETTER THAN ASPIRIN OR BUFFERIN" ... "THOSE FLAVOR BUDS FOR MAXWELL HOUSE COFFEE" ... "WONDER BREAD HELPS BUILD STRONG BODIES 12 WAYS" ... "THAT OLD 'FILM ON TEETH' CAMPAIGN OF CLAUDE HOPKINS" ... "COLGATE DENTAL CREAM CLEANS YOUR BREATH WHILE IT CLEANS YOUR TEETH."

You can agree or disagree, but this is a central truth of reality in advertising. The great campaigns, like the burning glass, fuse together all the components into a copy focus that generates not only light, but heat.

10
No More Room in the Box

In my study is a huge, old-fashioned pharmacist's scale, made of brass. The chains are heavy, and so are the great polished pans, yet the whole mechanism is delicately balanced on its fulcrum. Guests love to experiment with it; they tilt the great lever, as though it were remarkable that when one pan moves slowly up, the other moves slowly down.

The movement of these pans illustrates another principle of reality in advertising, and one that is virtually unknown.

One might assume that as the penetration of one brand goes up, it would have no relation to the penetration already bought and owned by another company.

There is, however, a definite relation.

As your penetration goes up, your competitors' tends to go down.

As your penetration goes down, your competitors' tends to go up.

Pause for a moment and reflect on this very thoughtfully. What we have said is that *you can actually decrease your competitors' penetration by using those advertising techniques and devices that increase your own.* You can actually cause the consumer to forget something he has previously learned by putting into his head a newer and stronger concept. You can actually remove an advertising story from his memory, and in its place you can substitute one of your own.

As you will see later, this will have considerable bearing on the kind of advertising you may want to run.

Nor do we mean that if you impress on the consumer something, say, about soaps, he will forget something he has learned about tires, or insurance, or automobiles. By and large, new penetration on soaps forces out other penetration on soaps; and new penetration on insurance forces out other penetration on insurance.

We do not know why this is true (why penetration on one product tends to force out only penetration on similar products), but it happens. One way to chart this is as follows:

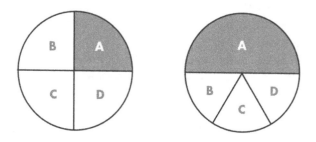

Here, four competing brands have equal penetration with the consumer. Each one has 25%. When "A" doubles his penetration, he actually decreases the penetration of "B," "C," and "D."

This is an important principle, and one that is worthwhile to explore. For students of advertising are likely to assume that penetration is an expanding universe, and that, as more and more advertisers come splashing into the market, people put more and more into their heads.

This is not true.

There is a finite limit to what a consumer can remember about 30,000 advertised brands. He cannot remember all the advertising he reads, any more than he can memorize the *Encyclopaedia Britannica*. What is more, there seems to be, in addition, a limit to what he chooses to remember about tires, or soaps, or cereals. For he has, after all, many other things on his mind—his work, his family, his home, taxes, money, friends, hobbies, sports.

It is as though he carries a small box in his head for a given product category. This box is limited either by his inability to remember or his lack of interest. It is filled with miscellaneous data, and, when a new campaign forces in more, some data are forced out, and the box spills over.

Do you doubt this?

Then, take one man and subject him to an exhaustive depth interview. Measure his total memory of advertising in any one field—be it cereals, razor blades, or beer. If you do this year after year, you will discover that the limits of his knowledge, or interest, are very finite indeed. You will be able to chart the size of the theoretical box in his head. Now, do this with tens of thousands of people. You will rapidly discover the size of the box against which we are all working—and you will discover that it is indeed a finite reality.

You will discover the reason for the short life expectancy of advertising, which we discussed a little while back. You will begin to see the tremendous difficulty of owning a bit of space in the box. For this box is, after all, the target of $12,000,000,000 in advertising money every year.

"There is no more room in the Ark," Noah, at one point, is reputed to have said. In advertising, certainly, there is "no more room in the box."

When a new campaign goes in, it must displace one that is already there.

11
The Beginning of Reality

"Let us count the apples now in the barrel," Abraham Lincoln used to say. "Otherwise, we may lose a few." A brief recapitulation is certainly in order, for we are now beginning to see the shape of reality in advertising, and a *procedure*, as well as a body of theory, is beginning to emerge.

To make our task easy, let us improvise a case history. Let us assume that we are a young manufacturer, with five very active competitors. Our business depends on advertising, but up until three years ago, our advertising had been based on pure "inspiration," with few facts and almost no tested theories.

Then we put into operation what we have covered in this little book, up to this page.

There have been, to put it mildly, some changes.

No longer are we making the mistake of equating our campaign, always, with sales. We are now separating out *the pure power of our copy*—without reference to deals, distribution, pricing, and dozens of other variables. We are doing this with national studies of penetration; and not just one study, but a continuing series of studies; and for not just our brand, but for all of our competitors' brands.

Now we know, *for the first time*, how many people remember our advertising. Even more important, we know just how well it is working—how many new customers it is winning over to our brand. What is more, we have the same data on all of our competitors' advertising. In a way, it is like sitting in on a poker game and knowing all of the cards in each of the hands.

Being aware that there is "no more room in the box," we have begun to sharpen our copy, to gather its energies together into that tight coil, for higher penetration. Aware, too, of the volatile nature of penetration—its almost vapor-like quality—we have stopped changing campaigns. Having discovered that a long-range campaign is worth a whole cluster of short-range ones, we are striving now for a campaign that can run for years, for we know that a good campaign will not wear itself out.

Our penetration is climbing rapidly. In fact, we now have the highest penetration in our field. As it climbs, we are beginning to enjoy a bonus that, before, we hadn't known to exist: Our competitors' penetration is moving down—as we seize a larger and larger share of the consumer's brain box.

Our three smaller competitors, let us say, are no longer a problem. One has a campaign that is producing no new customers. Another is even worse off: His campaign is actually depressing his sales. The third doesn't really matter—since he changes his copy, nervously, every few months.

We are learning, in other words, how to get that "extra edge"—how to reach much more surely, and much less blindly, for advertising's golden apple.

However, there are two worms in our apple, and they are very frightening ones:

Our two biggest competitors have stories far stronger than ours. They have far higher usage pull, and,

*even with lower penetration, they are reaping far
more new customers.*

Here is the crux.

What can we do about it?

How do we get stronger usage pull?

Here is the next part of our book, and we wish to
explore it thoroughly; for without stronger usage pull
everything else—facts, theories, high penetration,
even the most dazzling and enchanting of advertisements—may lead only to failure.

12
The Window Dressers

A study of hundreds of campaign profiles, over a long period of time, shows us that many of the most respected advertising campaigns in America are merely show windows.

Like the glittering windows on Fifth Avenue, they are spacious, shining with bright lights, rich with color, and often ablaze with tinsel.

But these campaigns merely display the merchandise. They merely present it to the consumer and ask that it sell itself.

Put yourself mentally, if you will, before one of the world's great show windows. Here are subtle lightings and superb arrangements, backgrounds done by sophisticated artists, so that the merchandise glows and gleams and beckons. Here is the ideal setting for a sable stole or a cerulean mink. A bracelet, designed by Schlumberger, or Cartier, or Van Cleef & Arpels, lets loose all its imprisoned fire on a gloved arm against black velvet. For T'ang horses, Ming vases, Aubusson rugs, old ivory, jewels—even shirts by Sulka, shoes by Ferragamo, or perfumes by Chanel or Schiaparelli—the show window is perhaps a sufficiency.

For these great luxury items, with their snobbisms, are not in our sense really "products" at all. The interest in them is almost inherent; they are the object of cults; and people buy them seldom if, in the mass, they ever buy them at all.

Now, strip all these luxury products and their snobbisms away. Put under this same glass the competing products from Grand Union, Shopwell, or A. & P.—mundane packages of detergents in their cardboard boxes, headache remedies in their tins, laxatives in their bottles. Add puddings, margarines, cake mixes, shave creams, toothpastes, and cigarettes. Put in the cereals, too—the lotions, the pet foods, the shampoos, and hair dyes.

Now, line up before the window fifty people taken out of an observation bus from Times Square.

The point will, perhaps, become so obvious that it needs no belaboring.

If these competing brands seem the same, what is going to make people believe that they are not the same? If these people do not know the advantages of these products, what, out of this multiplicity of packages, is going to show them the advantages? If their preferences are already set for one brand, what is going to persuade them to change to another brand?

Is the art of the window dresser a substitute for copy? Is it going to add persuasion?

Our figures show that advertising of this kind has no persuasion.

There is no usage pull.

In other words, the art of the window dresser may be the art of display, but it is not the art of advertising.

13
The Copy Leverage

From the dawn of history, mankind has been interested in leverage. "Give me a lever long enough," said Archimedes, the ancient Greek, "and I will move the world." "What's the leverage?" asks modern man, and, from the stock market to diplomacy, the question is at once a dream, a bandied phrase, and a glint in the eye.

So it is a natural thing to ask: "Do these researches show one type of campaign to have extra leverage—to produce more of this golden usage pull?"

The answer is: "Yes."

There is such a type of campaign, and it goes far deeper than the art of the window dresser. It goes deeper, too, than the mere facile art of the artist, the expertise of the art director, or the empty phrases of the wordsmiths. It goes, in fact, beyond all surface considerations—be they copy style, cathedral solemnity, soaring proclamations, humor, or even the most beguiling charm.

These campaigns have a U.S.P.

What is a U.S.P.? It is a theory of the *ideal selling concept.* It is a condensation—a verbal shorthand, if you will—of *what makes a campaign work.* Originated at Ted Bates & Company in the early 1940s, the theory of the U.S.P. enabled this agency to increase its billings from $4,000,000 to $150,000,000, without losing a client, while getting dramatic, and, in some cases, unprecedented, sales for its clients. It is the hidden secret of literally thousands of the most successful advertising campaigns ever written.

Today, U.S.P. is perhaps the most misused series of letters in advertising. It has been picked up by hundreds of agencies and has spread from country to country. It is now applied, loosely and without understanding, to slogans, slick phrases, strange pictures, mere headlines—in fact, to almost anything which some writers consider slightly different from what they find in competing advertisements. It is used with the casual looseness of Humpty Dumpty, in *Through the Looking Glass*, when he said: "When I use a word, it means just what I choose it to mean—neither more nor less."

Actually, U.S.P. is a precise term, and it deserves a precise definition. So we will begin by saying that, like Gaul, it is divided into three parts:

1. *Each advertisement must make a proposition to the consumer. Not just words, not just product puffery, not just show-window advertising. Each advertisement must say to each reader: "Buy this product, and you will get this specific benefit."*

This admonition, of course, has been on page one of almost every advertising textbook for the past sixty years; but as you will see, it is becoming almost a lost art, and more honored in the breach than in the observance.

2. *The proposition must be one that the competition either cannot, or does not, offer. It must be unique—either a uniqueness of the brand or a claim not otherwise made in that particular field of advertising.*

One might assume that a unique proposition, in itself, would be a strong theoretical base for an advertisement. However, there are thousands of unique propositions that do not sell. Witness, a famous toothpaste once advertised: "IT COMES OUT LIKE A RIBBON AND LIES FLAT ON YOUR BRUSH." This was a proposition, and it was unique. However, it did not move the public, because it apparently was not of importance to them. So we come to the third part:

> 3.   The proposition must be so strong that it can move the mass millions, i.e., pull over new customers to your product.

These three points are summed up in the phrase: "UNIQUE SELLING PROPOSITION."

This is a U.S.P.

At this point, we hear jeers from the wings. "What sophistry!" say a number of voices. "Here is a theory derived in terms of itself. First you set the objective of 'What campaigns pull over the most customers?'—and then you answer: 'A campaign that tells something about that product which pulls over the most customers!'"

The comment is not merited. We are not improvising a theory and cutting it out of whole cloth with a pair of shears. We are sifting out a pattern from thousands of campaigns and from accumulated masses of data. We are reporting what are the characteristics of the most successful campaigns. Nor are we making such a highly general statement. We are saying: "There is a certain type of campaign that delivers more leverage in usage pull. These campaigns happen to make a claim about the product, the claim happens to have the quality of uniqueness, and it happens to be a claim of an order that is of interest to the reader."

A copywriter who read the first draft of this manuscript said: "My God, *all campaigns* have a U.S.P."

Do they now, indeed?

Let us see.

14
The Tired Art of Puffery

A recent study of the advertising now running in our leading magazines shows that less than 20% of the campaigns have a u.s.p. This means that eight out of every ten campaigns tend to be what we call show-window advertising.

Let us pick up a magazine, and leaf through it, if only to sharpen our definition. As we lift it from the table, we glimpse the back cover, in full, glorious color. It shows Santa Claus taking a soft drink out of the icebox and smiling at the consumer. There is no copy.

Where is the proposition to the consumer? Where the uniqueness? And where the sell?

We turn the pages. Here, in a giant close-up, is a double-page spread of a man slicing a succulent ham. We learn, on reading, that "it makes mouths water" and has been "the most trusted word in meat" for 150 long years. Claims of deliciousness are universal in food advertisements, and the longevity of the maker is puffery, but not a product claim.

Where the proposition? Where the uniqueness? Where the sell?

We continue leafing through. Here is a big insurance company giving a salute to motherhood. Here is another insurance company, with a superb essay on George Washington. Here is a man passing an *hors d'oeuvre* to a lovely woman, and the headline proudly proclaims: "More power to please!" Here are five giant fruits (the macrocosmic is very popular in advertising these days), and we are told that these fruits have "field-fresh flavor, sun-ripened, a blend of tart and sweet."

None of these is a U.S.P.

Here a great motor car displays the usual stunning picture. We are told that it comes in "three magnificent series," as do most cars, and that it is "the all-time best, sturdy, trim, capable"—a little deluge of adjectives. A tire company tells us that "more people ride" on its tires than on any other kind. A beauty product tells us that it is used by the world's most glamorous women, but does not reveal why. A whiskey informs us that it is a "gift in good taste," which is, no doubt, a play on words. A beer promises to let us "know the joy of good living," which could apply to ten thousand products. A belt company simply flings its merchandise across a page. Three caramel sauces are depicted in enchanting color, and we are informed that they are "rich with true caramel flavor—really luscious!"

Show windows all, tricked up with the gold of the wordsmiths, but it is fool's gold. These are empty words.

A gasoline extols the joy of driving. So far as we know, the gasoline itself might come out of some great communal tank. Seventeen foods, and in virtually the same words, promise us "the best taste ever." Giraffes peer over packages, bears caper around food cans, packages are displayed against red velvet, crowns are placed on products, cakes grow to even more monstrous dimensions. Here a "masterpiece in art" is compared with a "masterpiece in a product." (There is an old saying in the trade: "When you don't have an idea, reach for an analogy campaign.") We are surfeited with slogans, deluged with pictures. Crisp but empty phrases of the wordsmiths crackle forth from every page.

But not one of these is a U.S.P.

We imply no derogation of art directors, photographers, artists, or the writers of words. Technically, these advertisements dance and shine. It is just that they have no real content. We find we are sifting through chaff and looking for wheat.

In the midst of all this, drop a real U.S.P.:

"STOPS HALITOSIS!"

The U.S.P. almost lifts itself out of the ruck and wings its way to some corner of the mind.

It made a proposition, when Gerard Lambert coined it back in our childhood; it is unique; and if it did not have sell, it would not have remained in print since most current agency heads were in grammar school.

We have said that campaigns with a U.S.P. produce usage pull. So indeed they do, but they also get higher penetration as well. For a study of penetration data makes it clear that mere show-window advertising puts no sharp, memorable theme in the consumer's mind.

Show-window advertising may make the name of the product, or the looks of the product, familiar to the public—but you very rarely see the message of these brands soar to 40%, 50%, or 60% of the national consciousness.

The reason is that these advertisements have no real message. They vanish into the underbrush of advertising. Written by copywriters who do not understand reality, they disappear into a fog of sameness, triteness, and triviality. Most of them have interchangeable parts, like a Ford.

"More people use . . . than any other!" "Tasty, tangy, tempting, appetizing!" ". . . adds glorious zest and sparkle to any meal!" "Pick . . . for pure pleasure! It's perfection!" "You'll be glad you asked for . . . It's incredibly smooth!" ". . . has never known an equal!" ". . . is the most in smartness, lightness, value!" "Flavor is king in . . . !" "When women try . . . , they go wild with joy!"

These are not parodies, nor are they body copy. They are headlines, selected from a single issue of a current magazine.

They are not advertising.

They are mere product puffery—anemic combinations of tired, used-up words.

Drop almost any U.S.P. into this world of gray sameness:

"PINK TOOTHBRUSH!"

The U.S.P. leaps out at you! And the result is not only usage pull, but high penetration as well.

15
The Three Big Roads to Rome

A scholarly German advertising man, who came to this country to study theory, said: "Your theories beg the big question that confronts modern advertising. Most products, today, are almost identical. You yourself are quoted as saying: 'Many clients throw two newly minted half dollars on the table and ask us to persuade the public that one is better.'" He added: "It is because *so few unique claims exist* that most agencies have begun to specialize in what you call show-window advertising."

This is a misunderstanding of reality in advertising.

It is true that a good many products are identical. However, even in the highly competitive package-goods field—soaps, detergents, cereals, beers, shave creams, breads, toothpastes, shampoos—the products often just seem identical. When an agency turns loose a group of qualified scientists, when broad-scale, open-end research and testing are started, it is astonishing how many radical differences come swimming to the top—differences either in the product, or in the use of the product, which had not been suspected before.

When this happens, the u.s.p. is often startling in its selling power.

However, there are three broad roads that lead to Rome, and finding a u.s.p. in the product (very much like finding a pearl lying in an oyster) is only one. Let us look at the other two highways an agency can travel when the products are, in truth and in fact, relatively identical:

1.   *The agency can induce the client to change his product, improve his product. We have done this on numerous occasions. A* U.S.P. *is thus specially tailored and built in —not only to the benefit of the manufacturer, but to the benefit of the public as well.*

A great advertising man of three decades ago once said: "A gifted product is mightier than a gifted pen." How right he was!

This is not a secondary road. It is often the first, and the best road, to travel.

2.   *If the product cannot be changed, and remains identical, it is possible to tell the public something about that product which has never been revealed before.*

This is not a uniqueness of the product, but it assumes uniqueness, and cloaks itself in uniqueness, as a claim.

The first two of these approaches are obvious, and either one can result in the best of all advertising campaigns. The third road, however, is something else again, for it may be filled with hidden subtleties and hidden dangers.

Let us look at a few examples.

Claude Hopkins, whose genius for writing copy made him one of the advertising immortals, tells the story of one of his great beer campaigns. In a tour through the brewery, he nodded politely at the wonders of malt and hops, but came alive when he saw that the empty bottles were being sterilized with live steam. His client protested that every brewery did the same. Hopkins patiently explained that it was not *what* they did, but what they *advertised* they did that mattered. He wrote a classic campaign which proclaimed:

"OUR BOTTLES
ARE WASHED WITH LIVE STEAM!"

George Washington Hill, the great tobacco manufacturer, once ran a cigarette campaign with the now-famous claim:

"IT'S TOASTED!"

So, indeed, is every other cigarette, but no other manufacturer had been shrewd enough to see the enormous possibilities in such a simple story.

Hopkins, again, scored a great advertising *coup* when he wrote:

"GETS RID OF FILM ON TEETH!"

So, indeed, does every toothpaste.

"Ah, now," says a critic. "Now we have you! For, when this U.S.P. is true of other products, it will become a standard claim. Other companies can steal your thunder and make the same claim."

Such objectors, again, do not understand reality in advertising. One of the realities is that such claims cannot be stolen by copy and copy alone.

Most advertisers will be startled by this statement. Actually, it may not always hold true with very small advertisers, with very small budgets, who never achieve any penetration to speak of; but it is invariably true in the field of the big, massive advertisers who can make bold, fast bids for national penetration.

Studies of great numbers of brand histories show that the first big advertiser can pre-empt the U.S.P. He is the pioneer, and, protected by his penetration bulwark, his is the reward. There is an important corollary as well: the first man in the field can rocket up with his penetration, achieving higher levels far faster, because of the newness and freshness of his story.

Thus, the U.S.P. becomes his property.

It is identified with him.

Who can steal "STOPS HALITOSIS" from Listerine? Dozens of other mouthwashes stop halitosis. Many tried to move in on this great classic U.S.P., until it became almost a source of embarrassment to them, seeking ways to phrase their imitation, so that they did not advertise the leader. This U.S.P., in the public's mind, belongs to Listerine.

Lifebuoy Soap made advertising history with:

"STOPS B.O."

All soaps stop body odor, and, for twenty-five years, many other brands attempted to crowd in under this tent, with phrases ranging all the way from: "It Protects Your Daintiness" to "Leaves You Fragrant, Fresh, Desirable."

None of them succeeded until a sensational, new product came on the market.

Colgate Dental Cream (long before it added its new anti-decay ingredient), pre-empted:

"CLEANS YOUR BREATH
WHILE IT CLEANS YOUR TEETH!"

One competitor sought to wrest this U.S.P. away with
a special, major campaign which proclaimed:

"FRESHENS YOUR BREATH WHILE

IT CLEANS YOUR TEETH

— BECAUSE IT

HAS A SPECIAL MOUTHWASH BUILT IN!"

It cost this company millions of dollars to discover
that it was simply advertising its rival.

The principle of U.S.P. pre-emption is an important
principle in reality in advertising, and it can be docu-
mented with penetration data, page after page.

What then, are the hidden dangers? The German
advertising man, at the beginning of this chapter,
said: "How simple! We merely take something our
competitors have never mentioned, and seize it." He
almost rubbed his hands as he repeated: "How very,
very simple!"

It is not so simple, and the danger may be found in
the text above where we say: "Such claims cannot be
stolen by copy and copy alone."

Here is the exposed flank. Here is where the manufacturer is vulnerable. For while *copy* cannot break a
strong pre-emption, a new and better product can. In
fact, a gifted product, properly handled, can break any
copy pre-emption, no matter how strong it is. Among the
immutable laws of reality in advertising is the following:

THE BETTER PRODUCT,

ADVERTISED EQUALLY,

WILL WIN IN THE LONG RUN.

The long run may take twenty years, fifteen years, ten years—or only one year; but unless the product has a *truly unique advantage,* as opposed to a pre-empted claim, it is vulnerable to the manufacturer who is willing to spend money on product development and put a dramatically superior product into the field.

In discussing the ways in which we arrive at U.S.P.s, however, we have neglected one important principle of reality in advertising. When we follow "the road to Rome" which deals with a real difference in a product—how wide should this difference be? How different is different? Can we build a U.S.P. around a minuscule difference, a tiny difference which may be in the product, but which it is impossible for the consumer, in actual practice, to distinguish?

Let us discuss minor product differences, for they are an important part of advertising success.

16
The Deceptive Differential

The theologians at the University of Paris, before the Reformation, refuted good sense and wore out the world's patience by debating, for years, how many angels could dance on the point of a pin.

They were eating, if only they had known it, Dead Sea fruit. So, too, does the advertising man who strains over minuscule differences. This is idea bankruptcy, leading to the distortion, exaggeration, fake claims, and hucksterism that have given all advertising a bad name.

We call this "The Deceptive Differential." We cannot tell you where it begins. Only good sense will tell you that. But it is bad advertising. It is bad not only in moral principle, but bad in its commercial results.

Writers who strive for these flimsy comparisons remind us, in a way, of Oscar Wilde's description of certain pink-coated gentlemen who ride after foxes in the English countryside: "The unspeakable in pursuit of the uneatable." For the consumer is led to expect something which does not materialize, which is dishonest; and because of this, the advertising has a built-in factor of disbelief and public rejection, which is stupid.

Let us go slowly here, for we are treading now on important theoretical ground.

The public (which has absorbed an enormous amount of misinformation about the advertising business) believes that an advertising man can tell almost any lie and get away with it. The exact opposite is true. Such a course leads, at the least, to wasted money, and at the most, to commercial suicide.

Alfred Politz, one of America's great realists in research, after analyzing the behavior of products and campaigns for many years, sums up this principle in two of the ultimate laws of reality in advertising:

> 1. *Advertising stimulates the sales of a good product and accelerates the destruction of a bad product.*
>
> *To make a claim which the product does not possess merely increases the frequency with which the consumer observes its absence.*

The corollary of this law is:

> 2. A *campaign that stresses a minuscule difference, which the consumer cannot observe, in actual practice, also accelerates the destruction of the product.*
>
> *Such a campaign again increases the frequency with which the consumer observes the absence of the claim.*

Industry czars cannot police the deceptive differential. It calls for the wisdom of Solomon and the powers of a court. However, there are 180,000,000 consumers who can and do police it right at the check-out counter. Such campaigns quickly yield to a fatal inner flaw, lead the public to expect something that the product does not deliver, and vanish into limbo.

With a major difference, however, it is another story. For example:

ANACIN is, and in a major way, quite different from aspirin, or aspirin with a buffer added. It is a unique combination of ingredients. Any physician, any authority on analgesics, will tell you that the combination of these particular ingredients has different effects on the human body than aspirin alone.

This leads to a valid U.S.P.

ROLAIDS is, in truth and in fact, far superior to its leading competitor. It contains a new-type antiacid, known chemically as DASC, which does let Rolaids take care of twice as much stomach acid as old-style alkalizers.

This leads to a valid U.S.P.

MINUTE MAID's new orange juice removes the water by a radically different process. Volatile taste components, previously lost, now reach your breakfast table in your morning drink; and Minute Maid is, as a result, better than any frozen concentrate ever made before.

This leads to a valid U.S.P.

None of these is a minuscule difference. None of these falls within what we call the deceptive differential.

They are the stuff and substance of good advertising.

17
The Emersonian Mousetrap

It was Ralph Waldo Emerson who made the remark that if a man can build a better mousetrap, the world will make a beaten path to his door. In terms of reality in advertising, this is a somewhat incomplete statement; for if the world does not *know* it is a better mousetrap, no one is going to make a beaten path to anybody's door.

Thus we plunge, directly, into the stickiest of all advertising subjects—the product comparison. It is a touchy subject, because an advertiser, if he has an advantage, must state that advantage; and often, as we shall see, he cannot make himself clear unless he states the advantage in terms of his competitors. Such a course invariably draws loud screams of fury from the opposition, even when the statements are true. Cries are made for "Fair Play!" Editorials are written on "Unfair Competition!" Appeals are made to federal regulatory bodies. This brouhaha has been going on, now, for years.

There has been so much loose talk about it, and so much fuzzy thinking, that any comparison has begun to assume an aspect of evil. Even some quarters in Washington have begun to sound the tocsin and cry that the Tartars are at the gates. There is talk of supervisory boards, vigilante committees, and industry czars.

"Product comparison!" "Competitive!" "Derogatory!" "Disparaging!" So runs the war cry. These are very loosely used words; and they are so often grouped together that many advertising men assume them to be synonymous. Just last month, at luncheon, a young advertising ass said proudly: "I will not work in an agency that believes in competitive advertising."

He should, then, quit the business.

However, since the terms are confused, let us see if we can put them in their proper perspective.

Our country operates (at least, we hope it does) on the belief that if a man can build a better mousetrap, he can and should make a fortune selling it with honest claims and at an honest price. The real question at issue is: "At what point, in describing his mousetrap, does this man disparage his competitor?"

Is he disparaging his competitor's product if he says simply:

"I HAVE A BETTER MOUSETRAP!"

Indirectly, he is certainly stating that others are not as good.

Or, into what area does he fall if he really takes off the gloves and advertises:

"WHY BUY OTHER MOUSETRAPS
WHICH DON'T WORK
ANYWHERE NEAR AS WELL? NOW COMES
AN AMAZING NEW-TYPE MOUSETRAP!
IT CATCHES 6 TIMES MORE MICE
—USES FAR LESS CHEESE!"

Or, suppose he goes even further and proclaims in no uncertain terms:

"MOUSETRAP CONNOISSEURS
ARE THROWING AWAY ALL OTHER
MOUSETRAPS BY THOUSANDS DAILY!
TODAY, EVERY OTHER MOUSETRAP
IS OUT OF DATE!"

We would seem, here, to be in the realm of opinion. At what invisible point, along the continuum that runs from mere product puffery to hard-selling, competitive copy, do we cross into the area of "derogation," "disparagement," and "unfair competition"?

We think the answer is very simple.

There is nothing wrong, or unethical, or disparaging in an advertisement which compares two products if the comparison is true, and if it conforms to just two conditions: *The comparison must not come within what we have called the deceptive differential, a straining to magnify minuscule differences; and the brand against which the comparison is made must be in major distribution, and not be some minor, unknown product, sold only in remote stores.*

Given these conditions, it is not a matter of opinion at all. It is a matter of fact.

If it is true, you can say it.

If it is false, you cannot say it.

The way in which you say it, if it is true, is a matter of copy philosophy, or taste, or your degree of selling enthusiasm.

But it must be true.

There is nothing wrong with what is improperly called "disparagement." It may, indeed, be *pro bono publico*, and the record is replete with cases in which it has been.

A final word:

Do comparisons make stronger campaigns? The answer is: "Not necessarily." Often they make worse campaigns, even where the comparison is a striking one. If, for example, you were advertising a car that could go 200 miles on a gallon of gasoline, it would be a pure waste of time to compare this remarkable vehicle with other automobiles. The facts are too well known. You would do far better to use the same time in describing your own car.

Consider the few campaigns that we have chosen to mention in this book. From "WASHED IN LIVE STEAM" to "IT'S TOASTED," from "PINK TOOTHBRUSH" to "STOPS B.O.," from "BUILDS STRONG BODIES 12 WAYS," to "FILM ON TEETH," in no case is another product even mentioned.

However, many products have advantages that can be made clear only with comparisons. If this is so, and you are clear of the deceptive differential, sing out the difference! Proclaim it in the market place! Otherwise you may rob your story of power and lose out in sales and profits.

18
No Bed for Procrustes

A legendary king, named Procrustes, had a bed into which all his guests must fit. If the guests were too short, they were put on the rack and stretched—at considerable inconvenience, we may add, to the guests. If the guests were too long, Procrustes had an equally simple remedy. He cut off their legs.

The German theoretician mentioned a few pages ago, whose personal tastes veered to the avant-garde, European school of "brand name surrounded by abstract design" made this accusation: "You are building a Procrustean bed," he charged. "Everything must fit a tight, rigid structure. It gives the creative man no leeway." His summation was: "Look at how u.s.p.s are put into advertisements. They are encased in hard, tight little capsulations of words."

Again, this is a misunderstanding of reality in advertising.

First of all, the raw conception of a great u.s.p. is the advertising man at his apogee, and it involves creativity of the highest order. Second, the u.s.p. is not something that is encased, like a larva, in a cocoon of words.

Think of a u.s.p. not so much as something you put into an advertisement.

Think of a u.s.p. rather as something the consumer takes out of an advertisement.

A u.s.p. is not a tight, closed structure. Creatively, there is no Procrustean bed. A u.s.p. is an end result. It is a totality projected by an advertisement. It is a fluid procedure rather than an arrangement of static elements. It is what comes through. It is what is played back. The creative man can let his imagination run riot, for a U.S.P. may be realized through a complex of visual and verbal elements.

It may be stated in words. Here is one that does just this, clearly, simply, lucidly:

> "WONDER BREAD HELPS BUILD
> STRONG BODIES 12 WAYS!"

Or, a U.S.P. may be put only partly into words. For example, the excellent Clairol advertisements say simply:

> "DOES SHE . . . OR DOESN'T SHE?"

In the context of the totality of this advertisement, the statement which is actually made to every glancing reader is a good deal more elaborate: "If you use Clairol, your friends won't be able to tell whether or not you dye your hair."

A similar campaign, with a classic U.S.P. which helped build an enormous business in a few years' time, was that of the Toni Home Permanent:

> "WHICH TWIN HAS THE TONI?"

Or, the U.S.P. may be a most fluid combination of words and pictures, such as the great Anacin drug commercial, with its three streams of bubbles flowing up to three boxes in the head. No one, as a matter of fact, has ever been able to sum up this U.S.P. in a tight verbal structure.

There are only three criteria:

Does the advertisement project a proposition? Is it unique? And will it sell?

If the advertisement can conform to these criteria, in strict theory, it can project a u.s.p. without using any words whatsoever. Johnson & Johnson ran a superb advertisement which showed an egg, stuck to a Band-Aid, immersed in a clear glass vessel of boiling water. If the claim that water, even hot water, will not loosen an adhesive is a good one, this advertisement would project the u.s.p. without words.

Often, in fact, by spinning a tight little cocoon of words, the advertisement becomes creatively too hard and too mechanical and loses some of its projective power.

19
The Freudian Hoax

I learn a lot from visitors from other shores. American advertising, being the largest and most highly developed, has become a Mecca for the growing industry on the continent. From Germany, France, Italy, the north countries, even Japan, agency men now pour into New York to study techniques and ask questions.

One of the surprising things is how many of them believe that American advertising men are employing deep Freudian techniques. They believe that we are manipulating people, that we have sunk pipelines down to the pre-Oedipal wellsprings, that we are practicing some dark, mysterious necromancy.

"But everything we have seen over here is so obvious," a number of them have protested. "What about the 'Hidden Persuaders'?"

Well, if these men did not find hidden persuaders in their own countries, they will certainly not find them in this one; for, as all top advertising men know, such talk is the sheerest nonsense. It may serve to make a best seller of Vance Packard's book; and it may pick up, along the way, people who are prone to believe in the sensational; but there are no hidden persuaders.

Advertising works openly, in the bare and pitiless sunlight.

We suspect this myth arises, and flourishes, because the advertising business has caught up within it so many diverse, brilliant, and highly articulate people. The terms fly thick and fast: "Freudian Complexes" . . .

"Hidden Motivations" . . . "Subconscious Persuasion" . . .
"Psychiatric Depth Testing" . . . "Psychological
Manipulation" . . . "Analytical Profiles." These voodoo
drums echo around a thousand conference tables every
day, until the mind is confused.

But, these terms are almost never defined.

Perhaps they are a symptom that too many advertising men like jargon. Or, perhaps, that too many ambi-
tious agencies are trying to create their own special
brand of client appeal.

They play no part, or at the most a very tiny part, in
reality in advertising.

It is true that no motivations are more powerful
than those deep below the threshold of the conscious
mind. However, these are dark, murky, and unexplored
seas—lit fitfully, in brief glimpses, by the flashlights
of the Freudians, peering into a darkness which mankind has just begun to explore. Some day, perhaps,
techniques will be devised that will enable advertising
men, *accurately*, to chart these dark waters, but, for
mass advertising, this day has not arrived.

It would take the reader of this book four years on an
analyst's couch to find out his own deep motivations.

We do not have couches for 180,000,000 people.

On our staff are specialists whose only job is to follow
all the developments in the Freudian field. We work with,
and retain, many distinguished academicians who are
pioneers in originating new measurements of this kind;
but it is a plain, simple, and very unvarnished fact that
*we have not yet reached the day when such research
techniques can be applied to population masses.*

"I do not risk my money," said Rothschild, staring at a reticent European king, "until I can verify the facts."

Good advertising men, like scientists, want research that is duplicable. That is, if the research is repeated, it will give the same results. An experiment that works one way today and another way tomorrow is very much like the drunk who is hanging on to a lamppost. He is depending on it less for illumination than for support.

There are one or two practitioners in advertising who claim to be in touch with the Freudian infinite. Like the Delphic oracle, they stay in business, we suspect, because people want to *believe* that they know the answers. We have tried them, and we find their reports vague, subjective, and as confusing as a hall of distorting mirrors. *Their findings, certainly, are not duplicable.*

Detroit, at one point in its history, paid an enormous fee for "research" of this kind. It revealed that motor cars were actually phallic symbols, and that people wanted them bigger than ever—rolling jukeboxes, flashing and glittering with chrome. The public, unaware of so hidden a motivation, proceeded to buy small cars by hundreds of thousands, costing Detroit tens of millions of dollars.

If you find this story extreme, we could give you many others. Sales of cigarettes and Life Savers have been attributed to the sexual symbolism supposed to characterize these products. A serious document, submitted to the United States Government, explained the unhappiness of coal miners in terms of complexes set up by their having to hack away at "Mother Earth."

A curiously shaped household utensil, which did not sell very well in England but sold very well in the United States, was again rationalized—and for a stiff fee—in terms of sexual symbolism. It seems that this utensil repelled the more frigid English women, while it attracted the more forthright American girls.

This is no way to run an advertising agency.

Over the next ten years, in this one agency, we will spend more than $1,000,000,000 for our clients. We will write thousands of campaigns. Like actuaries, we must deal with accurate measurements.

If you were a client, how would you rather we risked *your* money? On motivations we can measure, where the research is duplicable? Or, on motivations we can measure very imperfectly—if, in the mass, we can measure them at all?

It is quite surprising how much we can find out about what moves people. We can find out, within very practical limits, what people want in a given product; and there is an incredibly long list of *proved desires* out of which we can evolve a diversity of creative, and imaginative, campaigns. We know, for example, that we do not want to be fat. We do not want to smell bad. We want healthy children, and we want to be healthy ourselves. We want beautiful teeth. We want good clothes. We want people to like us. We do not want to be ugly. We seek love and affection. We want money. We like comfort. We yearn for more beautiful homes. We want honesty, self-respect, a place in the community. We want to own things in which we can take pride. We want to succeed in our jobs. We want to be secure in our old age.

The list of proved desires can be expanded, page after page; and here again you are staring at reality in advertising, for these are not gambles and speculations, but the very stuff and substance out of which great campaigns are made.

How do you want to sail your boat? Through well-charted waters, where beacons flash to mark the shoals? Or do you want to risk all on still-unknown seas—where you may bring home a rich cargo, but are far more likely to founder?

20
The Madison Avenue Lure

Once again we hear that voice from the wings, and this time it has a sharply accusing tone: "You," it says, "are denying the value of *motivational research!*"

We certainly do not want to commit this unspeakable Madison Avenue sin, so let us hastily utter a disclaimer: "Many U.S.P.s are arrived at through motivational research!"

However, let us define this highly controversial term, for like a brightly colored lure—brilliant with lacquer and gay with feathers—it is now being burbled through Madison Avenue waters to tempt the unwary.

Too many agencies have set up motivational research as a mysterious new tool, a new secret weapon. They have surrounded it with abracadabra. Writers, without defining it, confuse it with the Freudian deep-diving, and again we hear the old gibberish about hidden persuaders, secret manipulators, the plugging in on deep, irresistible, unconscious motivations.

Wrapped in mystery, the phrase is brought out like the Ark of the Covenant and paraded up and down Madison Avenue by a devout priesthood. What salesmanship! For motivation research is nothing more than an old friend who has gone to a slightly better tailor, grown a beard, and tried to disguise both his origins and his name.

The first advertising man who ever sat down to write an advertisement drew on his knowledge of motivational research. That is to say, he drew on his own knowledge of people.

What is it?

Motivational research is no more than a series of research techniques which have been known and used for years. Sometimes it is the depth interview. Sometimes it is the spectrum scale. Sometimes, the indirect question or any one of dozens of well-known, tried-and-true devices. All these are based on what psychologists have known for years—that if you ask a man a direct question, you may not get a direct and truthful answer, because the man may be concealing the truth from himself.

How many of us know alcoholics who do not know that they are alcoholics. Even when drunk, they will deny it.

Ask a thousand people why they smoke a filter cigarette. Nine out of ten will say: "I like the taste." Now, ask them why other people smoke filter cigarettes. They will reply: *"Those other people* are afraid of cancer."

Thus, we learn more. However, this is not the analyst's couch. We are not diving, deep down, into the dark waters of the Freudian seas.

We are simply asking better questions.

The brilliant research man, Alfred Politz, puts motivation research in its proper perspective with a story. "A fine symphony orchestra," he relates, "had been playing for years. They had sixty instruments. Along came a musician who said that he had invented a wonderful new instrument. He called it—'music'!"

21
The Brand Imagists

In our agency, we have a rather formidable copy presentation. It takes a full day to deliver, and it documents, in rather exhausting detail, many of the copy principles in this book. We presented it recently for some of our trainees. They squirmed through the charts, which explained the laws of reality in advertising, and the moment it was over, they shot to their feet.

"What about brand image?" came the inevitable question. "Is not brand image in direct conflict with the theory of the u.s.p.?"

The answer is: "No."

The theory of brand image, as explained by its disciples, is not in conflict. It is a very valuable and charming theory, on which a tremendous amount of work has been done, and it deserves the closest attention.

Let us examine it.

The best way to examine brand image is to describe it first; so let us listen for a moment to its most persuasive and able defender, Pierre Martineau. By far, the best exposition of it which we have read is in his book, *Motivation in Advertising*, published by McGraw-Hill in 1957.

Mr. Martineau has faint, faint faith in words. He says:

> *"Advertising people assume that all Americans are involved with words on the same level that they are. But in point of truth . . . few human*

*beings are . . . skilled with words. Brought up
on an intellectual diet of Grade B movies, comic
books, sports pages . . . the average individual
is not equipped to cope with the professional
communicator.*

*". . . he has a deep distrust for the person
who is too skilled with words. The feeling is
that somehow . . . he is going to overwhelm us
with assertions that aren't really true. This is
expressive of our profound aversion for the fast
con man, the barker, the pitchman, the huck-
ster—anyone who is too glib with words. We
are repelled by him. His words have the flavor
of wet cardboard. He's nobody we can trust."*

The result, we read, is that advertising men put an "over-
reliance on word magic." We are "wrong in considering
copy, or logic, sacred." In fact: "Words more often than
not play a minor role in what is actually happening."
What is more:

*"Any copy in advertising is an argument. It
is literally throwing down a challenge to the
reader . . . saying: 'Let's argue about this.' The
human reaction to any statement of claim is
'Wait a minute! Who says so?' Built into copy
is the presupposition of rejection."*

So down with words! As an example of this, Mr.
Martineau cites the distinguished Marlboro cigarette
campaign, with its men of virility and their tattooed
hands.

He states:

"Writers assume that the emotive effects [in this campaign] merely support their sales claims. . . . This is nonsense. . . . The copy logic is strictly after the fact. It merely gives the smoker a few conventional supports."

What, then, is the secret of these campaigns? The answer, we are told, is that brand-image campaigns communicate with the reader in another way. They establish contact with the subconscious of the consumer below the word level. They do this with visual symbols instead of words, Mr. Martineau says, because the visual symbols are far more significant. They communicate faster. They are more direct. There is no work, no mental effort. Their sole purpose is to create images and moods.

Such campaigns present psychological realities, which are just as powerful as physical realities. No longer is a product just a "sweet brown liquid" or a "mechanical object." The product, transmuted by these subtleties, becomes "something pretty wonderful, draped with many activating and pleasant associations." It carries with it a "rich load of aesthetic imagery, emotive meanings."

To put it bluntly, the u.s.p. is the philosophy of a claim, and the brand image is the philosophy of a feeling. And the consumers, according to the brand imagists, will reject the claim, whereas this other kind of advertising leads them to switch to the product subconsciously, because of a feeling that it is best.

Such advertising, in other words, appeals to the consumer's third ear.

This is brand-image advertising.

Abraham Lincoln was once driving along a road with a friend, who suddenly pointed his arm and said: "Look at that beautiful black horse!" Lincoln, with a small smile, said: "Well, it is black on this side." We would like, if we may, to take a look at the other side of the brand-image horse.

So words have no power to evoke and move, indeed?

"OUR FATHER, WHICH ART IN HEAVEN, HALLOWED BE THY NAME . . ." "WE SHALL FIGHT ON THE BEACHES, WE SHALL FIGHT IN THE HILLS, WE SHALL NEVER SURRENDER!" "GIVE ME LIBERTY OR GIVE ME DEATH!" "CARTHAGE MUST BE DESTROYED!" "WORKERS OF THE WORLD, UNITE! YOU HAVE NOTHING TO LOSE BUT YOUR CHAINS!"

"The right words," said Lenin, "are worth a hundred regiments."

Men have lived for words.

Men have died for words.

Cities have fallen for words.

Words, too, can be geared directly into our motivations.

Words can bring a blush, raise a smile, start the flow of tears.

Much of the gibberish of modern advertising *is* meaningless. The petty striving to magnify minuscule differences, thrown into a slick Madison Avenue argot, does indeed have the flavor of wet cardboard.

But Mr. Martineau is wrong when he claims that people cannot cope with words. It is said that 10% of the people in America are functionally illiterate, and many never glance at a newspaper or a book, but even to this group, words can be emotive. You can say four blunt words, and a man will hit you in the face. You can tell a story, and the same man will burst into tears. You can tell a joke, and he will roar with laughter. A single remark can make him your enemy, or your friend. And as for the art of straight, pure, unadorned communication, who can misunderstand a headline which says simply:

"DO YOU HAVE TIRED BLOOD?"

The really valuable part of the brand-image theory is its emphasis on the visual symbol. In this, the brand imagists are quite correct, for no one denies that visual symbols can stir deeply buried tides.

Just as a line of melody can evoke hidden memories, just as Duse could read the multiplication tables and make her audience cry, so, too, can a visual symbol—say, the small shoe of a child long dead—cause a mother to weep. For we all have a third ear, and it does listen, whether we will it or not, to the music of drums that we ourselves can rarely hear.

So it *is* better to drape a product, on the nonverbal level, with as many activating and pleasant associations as possible. We simply say: *"The totality of the advertisement must project a Unique Selling Proposition, as well as a feeling."* Embellish it then, if you will, with gold, or sprinkle it with stardust. Drape behind it the richest tapestries of the nonverbal school.

We believe that a raw and naked u.s.p. is one extreme; and the richest brand image, which does not project a claim, is the other.

The great Voltaire, listening to a fiery orator attempting to sow some of the first seeds of the French Revolution, heard him out and then made a sage comment: "I wonder," he said, "what he was trying to say."

What you remember of an orator—his dress, his personality, his conviction—is brand image. What he said—that is u.s.p. Either, without the other, may be successful in itself, but the combination of the two can have overwhelming power.

Winston Churchill, a colossus of the twentieth century, combined both. Who does not remember his dress, his personality, his conviction—the short, bulky figure, the pink baby face, the rolling and sonorous English, the dogged tenacity, the great gesture of "V for victory"? And who does not remember what he said as well—his massive series of brilliant summations, sermons condensed into sentences, which summoned a whole people to a new resistance?

"Give us the tools, and we will finish the job." "I have nothing to offer but blood, toil, tears, and sweat." "Never in the field of human conflict was so much owed by so many to so few." "An iron curtain has descended across the continent." "Let us therefore brace ourselves to our duties, and so bear ourselves that, if the British Empire and its Commonwealth last for a thousand years, men will still say: 'This was their finest hour.'"

No, we cannot do without words, which are the content, and we would be foolish not to try for the image, which is the form.

It is admittedly difficult in advertising to achieve both these objectives, and you will often find that you have to choose either one or the other. But the best theoretical objective is to *surround the claim with the feeling.*

Two and two, in the most elementary mathematics, should add up to four. In this context, they may well add up to six, eight, or even ten.

22
The Law of Calculated Risk

We have established a devil's advocate in this book who keeps making rude remarks from the wings. Now we hear his voice again. "You just don't know how to write brand image," he says jeeringly. "Doesn't it work?" And he cites a number of highly successful campaigns.

Of course brand image works! And sometimes, it works dazzlingly.

But let us come back to the analogy of the croupier. As we watch the endless spinning of the advertising wheel, we are not concerned with creating an occasional sensation at the table. We are concerned with the laws of probability. After studying them, the wise man will get behind the wheel and let the probabilities begin to work for him.

A careful study of the U.S.P. *approach, the philosophy of claim, leads us to the conclusion that the* U.S.P. *works in a far higher percentage of the cases.*

For nearly a fifth of a century, the penetration data on most of the big package-goods campaigns have flowed through our statistical mill, and the figures are, to say the least, thought provoking; for out of twenty campaigns which follow the U.S.P. approach we find:

> 10 good campaigns
> 6 excellent campaigns
> 2 brilliant campaigns
> 2 failures

When we check on brand-image campaigns, however, or the philosophy of feeling, these figures seem to reverse themselves. We find:

> 2 good campaigns
> 2 excellent campaigns
> 2 brilliant campaigns
> 14 failures

For the brand imagists move in the ectoplasmic area of mood and feeling; and it is indeed dangerous ground. The figures given above, as research men say, are not stable; but the margin of error is narrow enough to draw some thoughtful conclusions.

In the reality of advertising, an agency's problem is not to write brand image. The problem, rather, is to *keep the creative people from writing brand image*—to insist that they think in those creative terms which may bring their clients the richest profits.

This channeling of creative energies, incidentally, is far from easy. An agency head put it well recently, in *The New York Times*, when he said: "Of course copywriters like to swing 'way out.' It's lots more fun out there!"

Great copywriting, in its way, is not unlike engineering. Engineering can lead to art, but when it does, the art must flower on top of dozens, even hundreds, of practical considerations. No one will deny that the catenary curve of a bridge is a lovely and sweeping thing. However, the bridge is built for a purpose other than art; it must conform to engineering principles; and we know that it will stand. A pure artist might design a much more wonderful and aesthetic bridge; but it might not withstand hurricane winds, or the poundings of thousands of heavy, eight-wheel trucks.

The writer, being human, would naturally like to define creativity in his own terms. He is likely to regard his client's budget as a canvas on which he can paint according to his own whim. He would be wiser to approach advertising more as a designer, say, of jet planes, who knows that the end result may still be beautiful, but that the plane must also fly.

23

The Two Faces of Advertising

When Dr. Jekyll drank down his smoking potion, a transformation took place: The face that stared back from the mirror was a face that was no longer his own.

Advertising campaigns need mirrors, too, because abruptly, and for mysterious reasons, they change *their* faces. They project a new message, one not put into words; and this new message may be utterly different from the one the agency or the client has in mind. Here is a startling and intriguing part of reality in advertising.

We discovered this in an unusual way. Many years ago we wrote a campaign for Kool cigarettes which urged the public:

> "BREAK THE HOT CIGARETTE HABIT
> WITH KOOLS!"

This was in the very early days of television, and we showed, spread across the screen, the links of a heavy iron chain. As the announcer said: "BREAK THE HOT CIGARETTE HABIT!" the chain snapped, with a sharp sound effect, and the package zoomed forward.

After the campaign had been running for a while, we sent out a research crew to get the penetration—to find out what was getting into the heads of the public. In not a single case did we get back what we thought we had written. What came back was:

> "YOU CAN CUT DOWN ON CHAIN SMOKING
> WITH KOOLS!"

We were running a different campaign. What came out was not what we had put in. Jekyll, quietly, had changed into Hyde, and the campaign was showing the public an utterly unexpected face.

This, of course, was alarming. Obviously, meanings could change. The U.S.P. could become twisted, distorted. In fact, new and unknown U.S.P.s could emerge. For all we knew, on every new campaign, we might be taking wild gambles with our clients' money, for penetration checks can never be run until the campaign is in print and on the air and has been running for months.

So a whole new series of questions was posed:

Can we tell in advance what a commercial plays back? Given two commercials, does one project the U.S.P. better than the other? Are certain types of commercials better than others? What do competing commercials really say? What secondary copy points does a commercial get over? Is it possible, perhaps, to predict penetration in advance?

Ted Bates & Company immediately established a theater in one of the most congested parts of New York, where pedestrian traffic was so heavy that we could work steadily with live audiences. Projection equipment was installed; research crews were trained. A technique was worked out where advertisements and commercials could be thrown on the screen, under controlled conditions, and we could establish the playback before the campaign was released.

For lack of a better term, we called this our Copy Laboratory.

In the next ten years, we learned more about reality in advertising than any of us had suspected. Our very first experiment was startling; so was the second; and as we continued these studies, a whole host of patterns began to emerge and shape themselves into principles which began to appear as laws of reality in advertising. The first of these principles is: *An advertiser can be running two different campaigns—and not know it.*

Consider the story just told of the breaking chain and Kool cigarettes. This iron chain, put so casually across the screen, had caused something very strange to happen. A sea change had taken place: the combination of words and pictures was projecting an utterly different u.s.p. Let us suppose that we had written a second commercial using, say, a rope and had run them both in rotation. We would have been using two different u.s.p.s in the same campaign—both sharply different.

The penetration consequences are obvious, for it is a serious mistake for an advertiser to run two different campaigns at the same time. Yet continuing tests showed that many advertisers, all unaware, are doing this day after day.

For example, when a print campaign is adapted to television, the commercial on the screen very often projects an utterly different story—without either the agency or the client being aware that a new, and sometimes radically different, campaign has emerged.

Do you doubt this theory of the two faces of advertising?

Then listen to the following:

A Case History

Recently we had to change the lead-in on a drug commercial. This was not an ordinary drug commercial—it was one of the great proprietary drug classics. It had been running unchanged for years; and it had swept a new brand up, up, and up, until it was the leader in its field, doing millions of dollars a year in volume and in profits.

This lead-in was only seven seconds long, on a sixty-second commercial. Any copywriter would tell you that writing another lead-in was a simple enough job. A new opening? And in only seven seconds? Why, that could be done in a morning!

Indeed?

It took us six months.

We discovered that the new seven-second opening utterly transformed a golden drug U.S.P. into a leaden clinker—even though the rest of the commercial, all fifty-three seconds of it, was the same. And that was not all. In addition to changing the U.S.P., this new lead-in created a new idea of the nature of the product: people thought it was a different kind of remedy, a specific one for a different kind of physical complaint!

It should be pointed out that such case histories are extremes. They are the exception—and not the rule. Most campaigns are fundamentally simple in their structure, and whole series of commercials can be written with the same meaning and efficiency.

However, millions of dollars are risked on campaigns, and the agency cannot afford to gamble. In the case of the drug commercial mentioned above, the second face of this campaign could literally have ruined the brand.

What is the net?

If a client has a great basic campaign or commercial, it would be folly for him to change it unless he knows it projects the same u.s.p.

It would be equal folly for him to change it unless he knows it lodges this u.s.p. in just as many heads.

24
The Good and the Awful

Someone once defined advertising as: "The art of moving an idea from one man's head into the head of another." This is, actually, an excellent test of an advertisement. If one hundred people read the copy, or hear the commercial, how many walk away with the U.S.P. in their heads—sharp, clear, and memorable?

Advertisements, as you will see, differ enormously.

Ten years ago we tested four cigarette commercials. Each had the same U.S.P. What is more, the U.S.P. in each one was spelled out, in the same words, in one striking and very memorable phrase. However, the four commercials were written differently, using different techniques, so that we would get a pleasing variety. We had planned to run all four in rotation. Then we put them into our Copy Laboratory to test them against each other.

Here were the results.

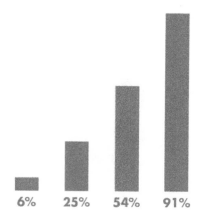

6%   25%   54%   91%

An advertiser who has not seen a chart like this, with his own commercials, should never forget it. For one commercial sinks the message home to only 6% of the people. The highest is 91%, or 1,500% better! It is fifteen times stronger—conveying the U.S.P., on a single hearing, to fifteen times more people.

Sometimes millions of dollars are spent on a single television commercial. If our client had chosen the worst commercial, using pure judgment, he would have wasted a tremendous amount of U.S.P. pressure. If he had run all four in rotation, he would still have averaged out with only a 44% delivery. However, when he took the best commercial and ran it until he developed others equally good, he wound up way ahead.

Again, the penetration consequences are obvious. A U.S.P. can work only when it is planted firmly in a head. The more heads, the more penetration—and the more penetration, the more people who will yield to your usage pull and be drawn over to your brand.

A word of warning, however, at this point:

Just because the Copy Laboratory can pick the most effective *commercial*, do not make the mistake of believing that it can pick the most effective *message*.

Time and time again, people ask: "But the Copy Laboratory *will* pick the winning campaign, won't it?" The answer is "No." The Copy Laboratory can pick the commercial or print advertisement which projects the message most forcefully, but it does not tell whether the message will sell. It measures only the powder charge, not the bullet. It measures only the effectiveness of advertising as a transmission belt, i.e., into how many heads, on a single hearing, it can move the U.S.P. Once the advertisement is out, or the commercial is on the air, it may prove to have a weak U.S.P., or a strong U.S.P. We have no positive way of telling in advance.

Some advertising agencies, and some research firms, state that they have devices for "predetermination;" but then, there is a great deal of nonsense peddled up and down Madison Avenue. "If I had such a method," Albert Lasker once said, "I could quit the business and make myself a million dollars a day." Do not believe an advertising agent who tells you he has a foolproof method. He is like the man who wants to sell for $100 a machine that makes authentic $20 bills.

Napoleon was once asked, at St. Helena, the secret of his very remarkable success in picking the marshals who led his armies. His answer was: "I did not pick them. They were selected for me by the God of Battles." So it is with campaigns. The great ones emerge victorious from battles. Put them out in test markets, get distribution, and run the campaign. Even then, because of variables, you cannot be certain what will happen in a coast-to-coast operation. That, too, is reality in advertising.

A subsidiary point on these live-audience tests:

Theoreticians may say: "The test commercial is heard only once. It is heard, too, under artificial conditions. Such tests do not prove how the commercial will project the U.S.P. when it is seen again and again on the air. Research of this kind may lead to sledgehammer techniques, which will offend the public."

Perhaps.

However, a commercial that obscures the U.S.P. on a single hearing probably will not improve, as a U.S.P. carrier, on a dozen hearings. Our researches show that the higher the commercial rates in these tests, the better it does on the air.

As for the so-called sledgehammer and repetitive techniques, we are going to discuss those now.

25
How Repetitive Is Repetitive?

Samuel Johnson once, in an English drinking house, leaned over to Boswell and said: "Do you see that scoundrel coming into the room?"

"Do you know him?" asked Boswell.

"No," said Johnson. "If I did, I would not think he was a scoundrel."

So it is, perhaps, with the repetitive commercial. A little acquaintance with this scoundrel, and you may not think he is a scoundrel at all. At least, you should understand him; for he is a part of reality in advertising, and he is going to be around for a long, long time.

Repetitive commercials draw loud screams of pain from the lay critics of advertising, and many tongue-cluckings from the trade press, which ought to know better. Often the lay critics and the trade press are indistinguishable: Recently one of our leading trade magazines employed a prominent critic of the arts to write a series of articles telling advertising professionals, and in no uncertain terms, how to run their business.

Apart from the fact that it might have been equally wise to ask a drug manufacturer to write an essay on the metaphysics of Jean Paul Sartre, or the impact of Salvador Dali on modern art, let us leave the critics for a moment.

Let us consider the case of a struggling package-goods manufacturer, seeking to exist under the American system of free enterprise and spending $1,000,000 a year on advertising:

A Case History
This manufacturer had four stronger, and big-
ger, competitors. Their combined advertising
budgets amounted to $22,000,000 a year. Their
products were good, and their money leverage
was immense.

To meet them, our manufacturer had less than
5% of the total advertising dollars.

For years, he had operated on the unreality
fringe in advertising. He had experimented with
soft copy, with pure brand image (dangerous,
as we have explained), changed campaigns, and
then changed again. Slowly, as most package-
goods advertisers do, he groped his way to what
might be termed "reality sell."

A series of experiments developed for him a
powerful u.s.p. *As he began to use it, penetration*
began to soar, and total sales began to climb.

A further series of experiments developed one
striking commercial for him, which not only
projected the u.s.p. *properly, but conveyed it,*
on a single hearing, to 82% of the people.

Within three years, his penetration climbed
from 7% to 44%. Sales tripled. The same com-
mercial continued to run over and over again.

Meanwhile, behind the scenes in test mar-
kets, this manufacturer was striving for better
u.s.p.s. *At the same time, he was testing other*
commercials on his original u.s.p.*, hoping for*
a still stronger presentation of his story. After
three years, and some $500,000 in regional and

copy laboratory tests, he was unsuccessful on both counts.

Sales, however, had soared from $2,000,000 to $9,000,000 and were still going up; and the same commercial, like a rich oil well, was still pumping out profits.

To which the critics of the arts, using the trade press and applying unrevealed and highly subjective criteria, possibly aesthetic, wrote: "Monotonous . . . repetitive . . . a pure lack of imagination . . . an imposition on the American public and bad business as well."

How repetitive is repetitive?

We do not have an opinion on this. Instead, for the critics of advertising, we have some rather surprising facts.

For fifteen years, at regular intervals, in forty-eight states and in hundreds of individual counties, we have steadily cross-examined thousands of people to find out what advertising they have seen, and what advertising they remember.

What is more, we have measured only leading advertising campaigns. In this study, the average expenditure is approximately $5,000,000 a year.

While a few commercials do reach an enormous number of people, we find that, on the average, seven out of ten people are not even aware of having seen the advertising at all.

It is possible, if one is interested in facts, to conclude that advertising men, and the critics of advertising, are much more sensitive to this "problem" than the public at large.

26

The Vampire Claim

Here is our old friend, the "Principle of Copy Focus," in a new guise—made clearer, sharper, and more meaningful under the lens of the Copy Laboratory.

We have seen, earlier, that campaigns with the highest penetration are the ones that present the reader with one moving claim, or concept, which he can easily remember. This does not mean, as we pointed out, that the campaign may not say many other things about the product; for secondary claims can add depth, color, dimension, and persuasiveness to the U.S.P.

Now, however, storm signals begin to go up. A red light begins to flash. We get a "Warning!"—pointing to the way this must be done.

In essence, the warning is this:

Be cautious, in the course of adding secondary claims, that a distraction claim does not suddenly crystallize, i.e., a second claim which sucks power away from your U.S.P.

We have found, for example, that if a story is remembered clearly by 60% or 70% of the panel, this story can be counted on to register strongly when it is put on the air. However, if the registration drops to 25% or 30%, the claim will not be able to make itself heard under normal viewing conditions.

Sometimes a second claim suddenly transforms itself into a distraction claim. Like a vampire, it feeds on the blood of the major story, bringing it down below the point of major registration.

A Case History
An important advertiser was giving one of our clients a very hard time. This advertiser had a potent u.s.p., and tests showed that he had an equally potent commercial. This commercial registered his u.s.p. with 69% of the people exposed to it in the Copy Laboratory—an extraordinarily good showing.

Over the years, his national penetration, out in the market, had built up to 38%.

Then, his agency decided to strengthen his copy. They added a second story. No doubt, having done this, they dusted off their hands and said: "Now this commercial really has power."

In the Copy Laboratory, this new story registered with 35% of the people. The old story, to feed this new addition, dropped from 69% to 40%.

This was a significant drop, bringing both stories down below what we call the point of major registration.

What happened in the market? One year later, when we checked the national penetration on the old story, it had dropped from 38% to 26%—a drop of almost a third. The new story, in the meantime, had failed to get much into anybody's head. It came in at a dismal 3.8% penetration level.

These vampires, these distraction claims, in other words, feed on the blood of the major claim, weakening it and sapping its strength. Yet, they themselves do not grow to full strength.

Again, let us go slowly, for we are covering important ground.

The illustration above is clean-cut and simple, for it shows only two claims struggling for mastery. Sometimes three, four, or five claims—all unrelated, and all clashing—are shut within the confines of a single advertisement.

Consider the following story:

A Case History
Recently one of America's biggest package-goods manufacturers, who for years had featured a single U.S.P.*, decided to meet all the claims of all its competitors* in one single campaign. *Accordingly, this advertiser introduced not one,* but seven *unrelated claims.*

One claim discussed a vaunted ingredient; another, a secondary use of the product; a third, still another use of the product. A fourth claim was built around a bactericidal advantage not connected to the first three; a fifth claim stressed the taste; a sixth claim dwelled on the advantages of the package; and all this mélange *was capped by still a seventh "claim"—a paean to the product's popularity.*

As a result, what had been one pure, clear advertising call gave way to a series of pygmy

voices, each joining in a confusing copy med-
ley. Recall of the commercial was shattered and
fragmented—none of these claims getting above
17%, and most as little as 4%, 7%, 9%.

The important theory here is that seven claims—or
seventeen claims—can be combined, and with tre-
mendous power, if they are not vampire claims. In
such a combination, however, each claim must be a
structural part of the u.s.p. Each one, like the soaring
columns supporting some great arching dome, or the
flying buttresses around a cathedral, must serve an
architectural purpose. It takes extraordinary skill, in
juggling the elements in an advertisement, to maintain
purity of line and concept; but you will find such purity
in nearly all the classic campaigns.

But if vampire claim is bad, it has a first cousin which
is worse—known as "vampire video."

When we put both into an advertisement, we com-
pound the felony of audience confusion.

Let us look at vampire video. It is one of the most
common, and least recognized, errors made in modern
advertising.

27
The Vampire Video

Sir Laurence Olivier was standing at the footlights in a great play. His lines were crackling with the brilliance of Bernard Shaw, when suddenly, with a crash, a maid dropped a tea tray at the back of the stage.

In the patois of the theater, this is known as upstaging. Gone were the gestures, vanished was the art, and disappeared forever, in the minds of the audience, was the dialogue.

What was remembered was the dropping of the tea tray.

Sandbags, for centuries, have been dropped on actors' heads for less; and yet today, long after the introduction of television, many of the professional communicators have still not waked up to a principle for which the Greeks had a word, back in the days when Sophocles was writing *Oedipus Rex*.

In television, it is known as vampire video, because again—like the vampire claim—it sucks strength away from your main story.

The aesthetic copywriter ignores it.

Clients are generally unaware of it.

Yet it can cripple a television commercial. It can almost completely wipe out, hide, or obscure the u.s.p. It can take $1,000,000 worth of television time and make it worth $100,000—or less. It produces commercials often dazzling in their art, but miserable as salesmen.

The television screens are filled with such commercials.

Let us look at some examples:

A Case History
A shining young girl, with a voice like a pure silver bell, once delivered a series of charming commercials. One night she would float before the camera in a bubble dress by Balmain; the next night, in a harem skirt by Balenciaga; the following night, in a tunic by Dior or Simonetta.

Men noticed her beauty. Women noticed her clothes. Only in the back room of the Copy Laboratory did a fact emerge which must be as old as Ur of the Chaldees. Most people could not remember what the lady had to say.

"How often," wrote Albert Camus, in *The Fall*, "standing on the sidewalk involved in a passionate discussion with friends, I lost the thread of the argument being developed because a devastating woman was crossing the street at that very moment."

We will see later the principles for avoiding these bright distractions and getting maximum registration. These principles, we must warn you, often lead to commercials considered by some people to be much less imaginative. But first, let us look at another case history, and see how vampire video can cripple a brand:

A Case History
Some years ago, we introduced a brand-new product on the market. This new product had

one dominant competitor, who for years had snored gently away. No intruders had disturbed his slumbers, until we arranged a rather rude awakening. We put on the air a commercial written according to the principles in this book. It was factual. It was positive. It had a powerful u.s.p., and tests showed that this u.s.p. registered with 80% of the public. It minced no words and burned in its story.

The defending commercials were something else again, and the following one was typical. It opened with a girl in a brief white bathing suit, posed high on a springboard. She was exquisite, lithe, young; and the sunlight sparkled on her as she dropped through the air in a swan dive. The water, in slow motion, cascaded up in liquid silver droplets; and, as the girl came out of the pool, the camera moved slowly up the dripping figure.

The announcer, during this sequence, was talking about the product; for the girl, in this wonderful scheme of things, was going to use the product, which had nothing to do with pools, dives, or brief white bathing suits.

The penetration was 65% on the girl. It was less than 10% on the u.s.p. A whole series of commercials like this was run; and meanwhile our commercial, unchanged, was driving home its message.

It was not long before the new product passed its older competitor and became the leader in its field.

How this company paid for some copywriter's fancy, some art director's dream! The approximate odds against their story, in terms of penetration, were about six or seven to one.

This is vampire video.

Sir William Osler, the great physician, describes one of mankind's most infamous diseases as "The Great Deceiver," because it parades under a series of subtle masks and disguises. So, too, does vampire video.

Sometimes vampire video is wrongly used animation. (Some copywriters have a compulsion to entertain.) Sometimes it is boys and girls on water skis, or dancers whirling to a fast rhythm around a giant package, or pure animated abstractions done eight to a bar. Sometimes it is nothing more damaging than a charming family doing absorbing things, but drowning out the message about soap, or insurance, or margarine.

Sometimes vampire video is a quartet, shown on the screen while they are singing a jingle. This could be excellent, if you are in the business of booking quartets. Sometimes it may simply be a famous comedian, doing an integrated commercial, but attracting more attention to himself than to his message. Sometimes it may be puppets, improperly used, hiding a golden U.S.P. behind their own winsome charm.

Often vampire video is as inconspicuous as a piece of jewelry on the hand that is holding the package, or a glossy Labrador retriever sitting in the front seat of an exciting new car.

Sometimes—hundreds of times, thousands of times—vampire video is merely the announcer on the screen. The announcer, today, is usually a vestigial remnant of the old radio days. Once a pure, clear, disembodied voice, he is now likely to be simply an intrusion on a medium that has richer and deeper dimensions. People will watch his looks, his clothes, the elegance or lack of it with which he takes down a book, lights a cigarette, or pours a beer. He may be working for scale; but scale, plus residuals, is more often than not merely the down payment on a far larger price.

Some copywriters actually defend commercials like these. They say: "It gives the public a *feeling* about our product."

Perhaps.

We have agreed with the brand imagists that feeling is a valuable commodity, but feeling cannot be added with a complete disregard of reality in advertising. When it is, the price of the feeling is often the sales message.

You have only to test commercials like these, measure them with the yardstick of reality, and you will see for yourself.

28
The Advertising Tool

Three thousand years ago, the Chinese coined one of the most ancient of clichés: "One picture is worth a thousand words." In terms of reality in advertising, this can now be rewritten:

"One wrong picture can steal a thousand words."

Here is the principle which makes possible the phenomenon of vampire video. Show a giant missile rising from its launching pad on a cloud of billowing, flaming gas. On the sound track, have an announcer talking about the wonders of your shave cream. We now know what the penetration may be. It may be 75% on the missile,—and 25% on the shave cream.

Or, show those glowing youngsters on their water skis while the announcer is talking about your beauty soap.

Pictures like these become vampire video because they have nothing to do with the words. The mind is split between missiles and shave cream, between young people on water skis and beauty soaps.

A dichotomy exists; and the picture wins every time.

Vampire video, like "The Great Deceiver," appears in so many guises that it is difficult to recognize. Recognition of it, in fact, is pure skill. It can only be learned by watching thousands of commercials go into a Copy Laboratory, and analyzing the results. Then, patterns begin to emerge and shape themselves into basics.

Here are three of these basics—dry as dust, as we sum them up—but fascinating when we begin to explore their implications: (1) Lock the video to the audio. Let the consumer see with his eye what he is hearing with his ear. (2) Put the announcer's voice under. (3) Seek for a specific video interpretation of the U.S.P. When you begin to apply these basics, much of the nonsense will disappear.

For example, sit down before your television screen tonight, and play the game of spotting the pictures that do not go with the words. You will be astonished at the large number.

Now, try locking the audio to the video. Does the voice say: "THIS TABLET DISSOLVES INTO 10,000 TINY BUB-BLES?" Then, *show* the tablet dissolving into 10,000 tiny bubbles. When you construct a commercial this way, you will find the useless picture rapidly disappearing; or else, in an attempt to keep the useless picture, you will find yourself writing some rather useless words.

A variant of this is the second basic: "Put the voice under." You will find, actually, that you are forced to do so when you try to put real pictures with the audio. In other words, get rid of that announcer holding the package and talking earnestly. This is an old radio technique, and we are dealing with television. What does his physical presence add? Is he not still vampire video? Of course he is! So, keep his useful words on the sound track and devise useful pictures to accompany them on the screen.

But the third basic is the most important of all: *"Seek for a specific video interpretation of the* U.S.P.*"*

Earlier we made it clear that a u.s.p. is not always a static set of words, a tight verbal structure. It may be an end result, a totality projected by a complex of elements. However, it often *is* summed up in words—a single, verbalized, unique, and powerful claim. Where this is so, we are discussing a keystone in an arch, without which all the other stones will fall.

Now we need something to bring the bones and stones of this verbalization to life. We need to find for the u.s.p. a video brilliancy of enormous power and clarity—a pictorial flash, like a burst of heat lightning, to illuminate the central concept. There will be other pictures in the commercial, illustrating secondary claims, which add dimension and depth, or, which add Mr. Martineau's mood and feeling. But these will swing out from this u.s.p. video like a man's cape swings out from his shoulders.

Once arrived at, this u.s.p. video will become a *sine qua non* of your reality campaign. It is not something you will give up lightly, and you may not wish to change it for years.

Let us look at a few examples:

The Hair Tonic

A hair tonic has a u.s.p. which states that it is less greasy than its competitors. In the audio, of course, this u.s.p. is stated in words, but in the video it is stated with even more force.

The backs of two men's heads are shown— one using the advertised product, the other the competitor's. Two lovely feminine arms are shown in spotless white elbow-length gloves. They stroke the back of each head.

One glove comes away smudged and greasy.
The other turns into the camera to show that it
is still pristine, spotless, and white.

With such video, it hardly matters who writes the words. The picture has moved through the eye, into the brain, communicating instantly, powerfully, even to people who are not at ease with words. Do not confuse this with show-window advertising, which merely displays an empty picture of the product, and do not confuse this with Mr. Martineau's visual symbols. We are not concerned at the moment with display, mood, or feeling. We are projecting a specific U.S.P.

Another example:

The Rice

A rice has a special milling process. Ordinary
milling processes strip away that part of the
husk rich in nutrition, rich in Vitamin B. Told
in the ordinary way, this story would have to
be told on the low-verbal level, with words that
would say: "We have more Vitamin B."

Instead, two grains of rice are shown. Along
the curving rim of each grain, above and below,
are lettered the words: "B VITAMINS." In one
sequence, a rasp-like instrument scrapes away
the husk, and with it, the Vitamin B.

In the other, two plungers come in from the
top and bottom of the screen, and the words
"B VITAMINS" are driven down into the grain.

A previous commercial on this story, done without reference to reality in advertising was surcharged with mood, feeling, and empty show-window pictures, but less than 5% of the people understood the product's very real advantage. The addition of this video jumped the registration to 65%. A difficult story, abstract and technical, became clear in a flash.

One more example:

The Toothpaste

A dentifrice contained a special ingredient which inhibited tooth decay. This ingredient was invisible, and the problem was: "How to find a video brilliancy for something that could not be seen."

A father was shown standing with his arms around his wife and child. Forty feet behind this group, a husky athlete kicked a football. The football swam up in slow motion, turning over and over, getting larger and larger. Just as it seemed that it would strike the man in the face, it hit an invisible sheet of glass and bounced back.

The man turned, rapped on the still invisible glass, and said: "Just as this invisible shield protected me and my family, so . . ."

In an unforgettable way, and almost without words, these U.S.P.s were driven home to millions. The difference in the commercial may be only ten seconds, or twelve seconds, in a one-minute strip of film, but as the French say: *"Vive la différence!"* Such story-telling pictures can be worth millions of dollars in sales and profits.

Copywriters of a certain kind shudder and say: "But my beautiful action and motion and verve and beauty are gone." It is only because they were looking for the wrong kind of action and motion and verve and beauty; they were seeking to please their own egos; they were not seeking reality in advertising.

An advertising man, like a designer, must control and direct his brilliance. A campaign is not for the individual expression of his ego. It is, actually, a tool, and it has a functional purpose, which is the most complete communication with the public, the maximum projection of the message.

This is the true art of advertising.

Benvenuto Cellini, an exquisite worker in gold, was asked to design a salt cellar for Francis I. Millions today are familiar with its delicacy, the poetic, sloping curve of the golden shell upon the tortoise's back. However, it was designed to hold salt and stand upon the table of a king.

Cellini was also an engineer. Had he been asked to design a wrench which could turn an iron nut upon an iron bolt, we do not believe that he would have put a golden seashell upon a jeweled tortoise, or even that he would have worked with gold. We believe that he would have used a harder metal and designed a wrench not unlike that used by the mechanic of today.

It could still be beautiful, for many tools are beautiful.

And advertising, keep in mind, is, above all, a tool.

It is a tool to convey ideas and information about a product.

If you will apply *this* criterion to modern advertising, you will reject much of modern advertising.

29
The Most Dangerous Word

We approach now, and gingerly, the most dangerous word of all in advertising—originality. Here, without doubt, is the Golden Fleece for which all of Madison Avenue is seeking. Here, misty, distant, and infinitely desirable, is the copywriter''s Holy Grail.

Unfortunately, it has ruined more advertisers than it has ever made, for it has never been defined—and the searchers thus are never sure just what it is they're seeking.

Let us look through, if you will, some of the recent flood of advertising texts and see what they have to say on originality. "It is freshness," says one writer. "The components of originality are style, liveliness, and imagination," says another. "It is any advertisement which is different," says a third, but without bothering to say different in what way. "An original advertisement," says another profound philosopher, "cannot be defined—but like a great oak, alone upon a summit, everyone knows that it is there." All this, of course, is colorful, but it comes close to being semantic nonsense.

However, it is dangerous semantic nonsense, for it sends too many copywriters panting after what Claude Hopkins described as "fine writing," "unique literary style," "clever conceits," "the queer and the unusual."

If you doubt this, listen to the following story:

Recently, an advertising magazine asked the creative people of twenty-five top agencies to pick the three worst

TV commercials of the past several years. These men and women picked (*as the worst!*) two of the most dramatically successful commercials of the past twenty years. One had introduced a new product, and in just eighteen months had swept aside all competition—not only seizing 60% of all sales, but, at the same time, enlarging the very market it was taking over. The second commercial, in another field, had done almost the same thing.

The reasons given by this panel were almost as odd as their choice: "No trace of cleverness or brightness," said one writer. "Unoriginal," said a second. "Dull," said a third. "I am glad I did not write them," said a fourth.

And these people are advertising men!

And advertising men are supposed to be salesmen!

Preoccupied with "originality," writers like these pursue something as illusory as swamp fire, for which the Latin phrase, incidentally, is *ignis fatuus*.

This preoccupation with "originality," at times, leads writers to absurd extremes. Suddenly, one of the very few *truly original* advertisements will appear. It may be a great success. Immediately, these writers begin to imitate it—unaware that they are copying merely the form, rather than the concealed gears, pulleys, and mechanisms that the master copywriter has concealed beneath the surface.

Jean Henri Fabre, the great French naturalist, once made a study of the processional caterpillars. Blind and unthinking, they wove their way through the grass in long chains, each following the one in front of it. Finally, Fabre managed to turn the chain and set all the followers in a circle, each one following the other, in a rhythmic march that had no end. For days, they circled endlessly, until starvation set in.

Thus, in advertising, the originality fads begin their endless cycles. One eye patch (following the bold and correct lead of a David Ogilvy) breeds a succession of mere eye patches. One beard, on a Commander Whitehead, becomes a thousand useless beards. Men sit on horses backwards; they sip martinis against Sahara sand dunes; they wear evening clothes down into the Caribbean surf; they play white pianos on mountaintops. Two animated brewers, because of their entertainment value, start a chain reaction of useless animations. One great jingle becomes a burst of empty melodies.

Such devices, when they implement the copy, are not folly. They only become folly when they do not implement the copy, when the device itself is assumed to be a principle of advertising probability, when as Claude Hopkins put it, "the writers abandon their parts. They forget they are salesmen and try to be performers. Instead of sales, they seek applause."

Strangely enough, such writers have a pseudo-*rationale* for this striving after mere "difference," and they plead it with passionate earnestness. The illogicality of their argument is not obvious to them, and it is even less obvious to the public and to many businessmen. In fact, it sounds enormously convincing.

The argument goes like this:

1. *Advertising (not the product) must compete with a tremendous number of other advertising messages.*

2. *Therefore, the advertisement (not the product) must get attention.*

3. *Therefore, a given advertisement (not the product) must be different.*

Such reasoning bypasses the product, and, when it does, it bypasses the advertising function. It is a classical example of confusing the means with the ends, for if a product is worth paying money *for*, it is worth paying attention *to*. The consumer need not be shocked or entertained into giving it his attention.

The writer must make the *product itself* interesting. Otherwise, a great part of his ingenuity and inventiveness will be used in devising tricks which lower the efficiency of advertising, rather than raising it.

When these principles are ignored, the singers are not merely singing in an off-key voice. Frequently, they are singing with almost no voice at all.

Consider:

A very distinguished jury was recently assembled for the judging of the *Saturday Review* Annual Advertising Awards. It included the Head of the United States Information Agency, the Dean of the Graduate School of Business Administration at Columbia University, the President of the Committee for Economic Development, the President of Smith College, the Chairman of the Board of a great public relations firm, the presidents of two huge advertising agencies—a total of twenty-five leading educators, editors, publishers, teachers, and public relations and advertising men.

This group studied, and very seriously, the whole range of public interest, or "idea," advertisements.

They selected, as the best, a striking advertisement of a great corporation which, for reasons of its own, had decided to ennoble the teacher.

The illustration of this advertisement was a pure abstraction by the painter William Baziotes. To the artist, this painting represented the ancient cave paintings where the drama of teaching began. To the unsophisticated eye, however, it looked very much like a confused blot—straight out of some brightly colored Rorschach test. The copy was certainly simple enough. It consisted of twelve words from *The Education of Henry Adams:* "A teacher affects eternity; he can never tell where his influence stops."

Out of curiosity, we researched this advertisement very carefully. We discovered that it had two main drawbacks:

Exactly 100% of the people did not understand the picture.

Exactly 85% of the people did not grasp what the advertisement itself was trying to say.

Comments on the picture should make any theorist pause and ponder: "It's a picture of a tombstone." "It shows a crocodile eating." "It's a figure with its mouth open to the right, with a square worm over it." "It shows a cat lying on its back, looking up at the sky."

Comments on the totality of the advertisement were equally informative: "It shows what brings eternity." "What I get out of it is the universe." "It's just modern and pretty, I guess." "They are trying to sell some book."

This is not the science of communication.

This is the science of ex-communication.

Too many writers assume that mere "difference," "cleverness," the "queer and the unusual"—like the philosopher's stone, for which the ancient alchemists sought—have within them some mysterious essence which can transmute lead into pure and shining gold.

Unfortunately, lead remains lead.

We must start with gold.

30
A New Definition

In 1905, Albert Lasker—described by his friend, Ben Sonnenberg, as "an advertising man carved out of the side of a mountain"—was sitting in his office in Chicago when a messenger brought in a note from a stranger. It read:

> "I am downstairs in the saloon. I can tell you what advertising is. I know you don't know. If you wish to know, send the word 'yes' down by the bellboy."
> SIGNED—John E. Kennedy

This was the first appearance on the advertising scene of this remarkable man. Tall, strikingly handsome, and an ex-member of the Canadian Mounted Police, he was the first great advertising theorist. Most of his theories, set down by Lasker years later, are still as fresh and glistening as new paint on the wall.

Kennedy's first question to Lasker was: "Do you know what advertising is?"

"Yes," said Lasker, "I think I do. Advertising is news about a product."

"No," said Kennedy. "News is merely a technique of presentation. Advertising is *salesmanship in print.*"

The definition sounds primitive today, but, at that time, it was revolutionary. Some men had confused advertising, as they still do today, with great writing. Others were devoting their lives to finding clever slogans. Still others were content with pictures of the product. One big firm defined advertising simply as "Keeping your name before the public." Another stated that it was "Spending your money in the right papers"—but did not specify spending the money in what way. Another proclaimed "Keeping everlastingly at it brings success"—but did not say keeping at what.

Unfortunately, Kennedy's old and classic definition is not precise enough today. Too many advertising writers, who never sold anything, have their own definitions of "salesmanship." It is time for a new definition, in terms of reality in advertising.

We think it would be:

ADVERTISING IS THE ART OF GETTING
A UNIQUE SELLING PROPOSITION
INTO THE HEADS OF THE MOST
PEOPLE AT THE LOWEST
POSSIBLE COST.

If this is true, the problem of the advertising man begins to define itself, and in a very clear sequence. First, it is the creation of the right message. Here, actually, is the ultimate in advertising originality; for once achieved, a hundred men might write a hundred different advertisements, and each might be tremendously successful. Second, it is the writing of the advertisement *so that it projects this message to the maximum number of people.*

Now we see the true limits of originality. We see that originality cannot be wild, and free, and unfettered. It must, within the limits of advertising functionalism, restrict itself.

121 /

No longer can the copywriter, like Tennyson's Lady of Shalott, view life through his own magic mirror. No longer can he live in that state the saints call *Innigkeit,* or "inwardness." For him, no longer, can private planets shine in some solipsist universe where his delusions can be treated as reality. He must make his imagination function under the strict discipline of attaining a commercial goal.

Such discipline should hardly be bitter medicine. Even Beethoven's titanic hammer-strokes were based on the discipline of harmony. It may even be possible, within the confines of unpleasant practicality, to have beautiful pictures and colored clouds of soaring words.

"But . . . ," we hear the voice from the wings.

There are, unfortunately, no "buts." An advertisement *is* an instrument of commerce, and, like a diesel motor, it must be judged on whether it performs what it was designed to do.

Is a wristbone unoriginal or uncreative? Is an ear? Or are they beautifully functional—slim, like a needle, or ovoid, like an egg—*shaped the way they are because they have a specific function to perform?*

Does the tread of a tractor cry for the addition of non-essentials? The curve of a spring? A light bulb? A radar antenna?

We do not think so.

Our researches lead us to the conclusion that there are two extremes in advertising:

1. *Advertising designed as art, without reference to its business function.*

2. *Advertising designed for its business function—which may not be considered by some critics to be a work of art.*

The first should be viewed with suspicion, since it usually obscures the message.

The second should be judged by its results, rather than by critics who are concerned with aesthetics rather than with profits.

I would like to add a wry comment:

Only occasionally are great salesmen "things of beauty." They do not carry paintings by Picasso in their hands, speak in rhyme, or sing, dance, and play the flute. They are usually very earnest men, *who speak convincingly and with knowledge about why their product is better.*

31
The Best Way to Sow the Seeds

One of advertising's greatest theories can be summed up in the question: "What is the best way to sow the seeds?"

The seed, of course, is the advertisement; within it, fruitful and ready to germinate, is the U.S.P.

Do we sow these seeds profusely, and heavily, over a few acres, or, do we scatter them over a much larger area of ground?

Here is a key principle of reality in advertising; yet it is often practiced wrongly by many top agency men, veterans of decades of campaigns. They write powerful advertisements; they spend millions of dollars on them; and then they wonder, if they look into penetration at all, why the results are less than fruitful.

Put precisely, the question is:

Is it better to reach a smaller audience, yet reach it more times? Or is it better to reach a bigger audience—yet reach it less often?

To take an extreme example, an advertiser might be able to spend all his funds in two great magazines and one television show. In this way, he might reach 30,000,000 people—by and large, the same people—an average of three times a week. Or, might it be wiser to reach 90,000,000 people, say, once a week?

The answer, of course, is—buy dispersion. Try to reach more homes, not the same homes. Try to reach more people, not the same people.

In other words, reach your audience less often, but make it as large an audience as you can.

It should be pointed out that this theory applies only to mass-consumption products. It would be foolish to buy dispersion for, say, a farm tractor—or any product that appeals only to a select audience. But for products like soaps or cigarettes, automobiles, food, or insurance, dispersion is a necessity.

What led us to specialize in dispersion, incidentally, is in itself an interesting story.

Back in the early 1940s, we observed that certain brands were spurting ahead in sales. We began to analyze their activities, to see whether or not some principle, unknown to us, might not be at work.

Indeed there was.

We discovered that these brands were buying non-network spots or adding them to their other media.

This was puzzling, for these spots were not only costly, but they all fell in the daytime. What is more, they were broadcast between programs—thus missing out on a sacred fetish of many advertising men, the consumer's alleged loyalty to the show.

With the help of the A. C. Nielsen Company, we began to explore this puzzle. We took an average daytime radio spot list and compared it to an average fifteen-minute, five-times-a-week show.

We discovered that we reached twice as many people as the top-rated daytime show.

We discovered that we reached even more homes than the biggest evening show then on the air!

And this happened despite the ratings of the spots, for the spots that we analyzed were not better than average. What had happened was that these spots were dispersing the message, scattering the message, sowing the seeds much more widely—reaching a much larger audience, although not as many times.

Further analysis revealed that this principle did not depend on spots. An advertiser, if he had more than one product to advertise, could do the same thing with shows. He could buy different shows, of different types, in different times, on different networks or stations, appealing to different audiences. Then, he could cross-ruff his commercials, i.e., use his shows as spot carriers. The results would be golden. Penetration would mount up, up, and up. Sales would spurt ahead.

The ideal dispersion, of course, would be to reach 100% of the people and then repeat with as much frequency as the budget will permit. There is no such buy; but until an advertiser can reach maximum audience, 80% to 90%, he must keep reaching out for more and more different people. Then, and only then, should he begin to add frequency.

Keep in mind that this has nothing to do with the size of the budget. Nor does it dictate the choice of media, for it will work equally well in magazines, in newspapers, or in broadcast.

One way, the advertiser utilizes his dollars to the maximum.

The other way, he wastes his money.

Many great advertisers do not know this. For example, one of America's largest agencies tells its clients:

"Sell in depth. Take a smaller audience, and hit them over and over and over again."

Another agency took the entire budget of a big brand and spent it all in a single weekly magazine.

Watch your television screen. Soon you will find an advertiser who devotes an entire show to a single product. You will find three commercials, on one half hour, for the same brand. This advertiser would double his audience, and double his penetration, if he were to put one commercial on three different shows.

Notice that we said: "Double his penetration." This leads to a natural question: *"Does the principle of dispersion lead to higher penetration?"*

The answer is: "Yes." We have measured dispersion and checked it against national penetration, and, while the correlation is not perfect, there is an amazing similarity.

For example, we recently measured nineteen brands being handled by Ted Bates & Company. We found that these brands—some with big budgets and some with little budgets—were reaching an average of 37% of all homes. Then, we checked the public to see who remembered the advertising message.

Here are the results:

Audience	37%
Penetration	35%

Tables of figures are dreary things, but it will pay the theorist to study the following simple table very carefully. For, when we subdivided these nineteen brands, the figures became even more meaningful:

	Audience	_Penetration_
4 brands reached	16%	19%
4 brands reached	26%	26%
4 brands reached	32%	40%
4 brands reached	48%	36%
3 brands reached	70%	59%

The implication of these figures is obvious. The more homes you reach, the more heads you will get your message into, and the more opportunity you will be giving your copy to make sales for you.

However, it does not follow that these figures will work for all kinds of copy. This book has dealt with reality in advertising, and the copy we have measured has been reality copy. It is u.s.p. copy, sharply focused, run unchanged, often repetitive, with no distraction video, with strong video behind the u.s.p.—and with Copy Laboratory checks to make sure that no commercials with low-copy delivery are going on the air.

However, with reality copy, it is possible to calculate dispersion and, with reasonable accuracy, determine what levels of national penetration you can reach.

Do not seek for this correlation, however, with show-window advertising. And, do not seek for it with commercials that emerge from a Copy Laboratory with a copy delivery of 5%, 10%, or even 30%.

Dispersion sounds easy. It is far from easy. The average media department does not have, automatically built into it, the machinery and wide knowledge which can bring it about. Dispersion is actually a complicated and precise undertaking—a gigantic jigsaw puzzle, consisting of thousands and thousands of tiny pieces. Each one must be fitted neatly into place, and this calls not only for a huge media department, but one staffed with specialists in this particular field.

Today, when we find a brand that is failing to keep pace with its competitors, we look at its dispersion. A large number of times—far, far too often—this is the error.

Meanwhile, somewhere, puzzled men may be wondering why good copy does not always produce good sales.

32
Reality Sell

Where, now, do we stand on our body of theory? A summing up is in order; for we have not only covered many subjects, but we have been forced to put, in little chapters of two or three pages, some principles that deserve small volumes in themselves.

The best way to sum up is to take a typical manufacturer, who has been doing everything quite wrong, and see how this body of theory changes his entire advertising operation.

Let us introduce him:

He is a hard-working manufacturer with a relatively new company, spending $1,000,000 a year in advertising. Sales are down, profits are down, and his costs are mounting steadily. He has a good, but not exceptional, product. He employs 750 people, who support, in turn, about 3,000 people. This company is a youngster, so to speak—an example of free enterprise, in the free auction of the market, trying to get ahead.

Facing this company, however, are two dominant and much stronger competitors. One has 50% of the sales, and the other has 35%. They are spending $4,000,000 and $3,000,000 respectively—leaving our manufacturer with only 12½% of the total advertising dollars and only 15% of the total sales. This is enormous advertising leverage against his brand.

However, our manufacturer has not been making conditions any better, because he has been practicing, in its fullest implications, unreality sell. He has had no copy measurements of any kind and has been trying to judge his campaigns by sales, in a market filled with deals and variables. Even worse, he has changed campaigns steadily. For years, he ran show-window advertising. He dabbled in Freudian research. Then he experimented with mood and feeling copy, i.e., pure brand image. Most of his copy fitted what we describe as "The Tired Art of Puffery." Convinced, too, that his small budget could make no national impact, he has concentrated on a small audience, ignoring "The Principle of Dispersion." In ten years, he has switched agencies four times—but despite each new campaign, he has watched his sales shrink slowly, year by year.

Then he switched to *"Reality Sell."*

A national penetration check turned a blindingly bright, if shocking, searchlight on his copy operation. He discovered that his biggest competitor had a penetration of 36%, the other a penetration of 27%, and his own was less than 10%. What is more, each of his competitors had a fair usage pull—*but his own was zero!* In other words, the people who knew his advertising bought no more of the product than the people who did not know his advertising.

Now, however, he began to go to work.

He explored, thoroughly, "The Three Big Roads to Rome." He chose to improve his product, on the theory that "a gifted product is mightier than a gifted pen." This gave him, for the first time, a potent u.s.p. and strong copy leverage. In addition, it gave him a powerful product comparison and one way outside "The Deceptive Differential."

He began to see advertising, for the first time, as a tool. He applied "The Principle of Copy Focus," so that his U.S.P. began to sing out. He worked hard to make his campaign a philosophy of claim crossed with a philosophy of feeling. Audio was locked to video in his television commercials; vampire claims were eliminated; vampire video went out the window. He developed a striking central video to highlight his U.S.P. still further—like that burst of heat lightning which makes everything so vivid and clear.

Copy Laboratory tests not only helped him achieve these objectives, but, in addition, they quickly separated "The Good from the Awful." He emerged with a series of commercials, which, in the Copy Laboratory, projected his new U.S.P. into 80% of the heads. Meanwhile, similar tests showed him that his competitors' commercials had an average registration of only 30%, assuring him of an enormous margin.

This margin, however, was to be increased in still another way, for a market test revealed that his new U.S.P. had a usage pull of 18%—compared with 9% for one of his competitors and 5% for the other.

Simultaneously, a full-scale media study revealed that neither of his competitors was taking advantage of "The Principle of Dispersion." He rapidly overhauled his schedules, cutting down on frequency, and reaching out for more and more people.

Underlying all this activity was a new and exciting understanding of some of the broader reality principles. He understood now "The Life Expectancy of Advertising." He was aware that there was "No More

Room in the Box." He knew, now, that he had spent years chopping down his own trees, and that his past campaigns were but a series of hacked-down saplings. Understanding, at last, that changing a campaign is like stopping the money—and secure in the knowledge that his new campaign would not wear out—he was now making plans to grow, instead, a giant of the forest.

What an astonishing difference to his company!

Almost instantly, his new usage pull began to reflect in his total sales. Penetration began to climb steadily—to 16% the first year, 20% the second year, 26% the third year, 34% the fourth year, 39% the fifth year, and 47% the sixth year. During this time his competitors, out of worry, went into a not unusual reaction procedure—changing their own campaigns. This lowered their penetration just when they needed to improve it; and this lowering was accentuated by another advertising principle: his competitors' penetration was driven further down, as he seized a larger and larger share of the consumer's brain box.

The seventh year, his penetration was 60%, and that of his competitors was down to 22% and 18%, respectively. His advertising budget, geared to growing sales, was now $3,500,000—and from a very bad third, he was now in second place.

Barring accidents, and watching the errors his less expert competitors are making, he knows that, shortly, he will be No. 1 in sales.

A mythical case history? No. It happened. And we have seen it happen again and again and again.

33
Some Principles About Principles

When this book was being finished, it was read, up to this point, by a distinguished advertising man who had been a specialist for years in the field of automobile advertising.

"It is very interesting," he said, nodding his head, "what specialized principles you people have developed in the field of package goods. Most of them have very little relation to any other form of advertising."

How wrong he was! The principles of communication—or reality in communication—are universal in mass advertising. "Show-Window Advertising," "Copy Focus," "Penetration," "Usage Pull," "The Multi-Million Dollar Error," "The Two Faces of Advertising," "Vampire Video," "The Vampire Claim," "Dispersion," "The U.S.P.," "The Good and the Awful," "The Law of Calculated Risk"—all the many principles set forth in this book—can be applied to almost any type of product. They are above product, actually, and will work equally well for insurance companies, institutional campaigns, banks, ethical drugs, hard goods, soft goods, or gasolines.

When I made this reply, my friend shook his head. "Well," he said, "they do not apply to automobiles. For example, we could never have a U.S.P. You forget that we must sell a constant procession of individual features, and we have a brand-new product every year."

Well, these principles certainly are not being applied, for most automobile campaigns today are what we call show-window advertising, but they can be applied, for they once were applied.

I am referring to the great, historic automobile campaign for DODGE, run by Walter Chrysler back in the darkest days of the Depression. Chrysler took as his U.S.P. the theme of "DODGE DEPENDABILITY"—the toughness, ruggedness, and economy of this car. Conceived by Sid Schwinn, this campaign was worked out in a series of brilliant and superbly finished advertisements, rich with showmanship, which belong, if one is ever established, in some campaign Hall of Fame.

The first advertisement was a double-page spread. On the left-hand page, the car was shown plunging at high speed through a sandpit, with gravel sheeting up over the hood; on the right-hand page, the car stood, polished and beautiful, on the showroom floor; and the headline streaming underneath was:

"POWDERS HER NOSE IN A SANDPIT,
WINS HONORS AT A BEAUTY SHOW!"

In subsequent advertisements, the car was shown being rolled off cliffs to prove that it could still be driven away under its own power and to prove that the doors still opened and closed. It was sent smashing through creeks. Elephants were photographed standing on its top to show the strength of the body. Chorus girls, two and three at a time, were shown hanging from one opened door to prove the strength of the hinges. "DODGE DEPENDABILITY . . . TOUGHNESS . . . RUGGEDNESS—WITH

BEAUTY!" This was the U.S.P., although it was never summed up in so many pat words.

And as the campaign continued, year after year, model after model was introduced within the framework of this U.S.P., and feature after feature was forcefully made clear.

Far better than show-window advertising, this campaign continued to build penetration on a great single concept, a U.S.P. And in a time of darkness and panic, when cars were very serious purchases, it rolled up a 154% increase in sales *in the first year*, moving Dodge from ninth to fourth place. The second year sales took another jump—a rich 70%.

So the answer is not that the principles in this book *cannot* be applied.

The answer is that they *are not being applied.*

These principles were learned through package-goods advertising, and that is good; for package goods is a hard school, with huge budgets, rough competition, frequent purchases, and low unit costs. Fierce cats prowl this jungle, and the weak and foolish die, often without knowing why, at the water hole. Darwin's law of survival of the fittest is at work every minute of every day. Mistakes become quickly, and hideously, apparent. The principles of survival become crystal clear.

And these principles apply to toads as well as tigers, to moths as well as mastodons. It is interesting, in this connection, to note that the great Chrysler campaign was written by what was then a pure package-goods agency.

Just as these principles worked then for automobiles, so they can be made to work for appliances, soft goods, gasolines, insurance companies, or even the loftiest and most tenuous of institutional campaigns.

All one has to do is apply them.

34
The Madison Avenue Myth

"A myth," Arnold Toynbee once remarked, "is a curious animal; for it feeds upon itself, and the more it eats, the larger it grows." A giant of the species now crouches above Madison Avenue. It is swollen, already, to monstrous proportions, and every day its dimensions are puffed up still further.

This myth deals with the powers of the advertising man.

We are not concerned here with the advertising man of the novelists and the Sunday supplements. This apparition dresses in gray flannel suits; his diet is gin; his hobby is adultery; his vocabulary is jargon; and his intelligence—if all these things are true—is not too high.

We are concerned, instead, with the advertising man of the new economists and such writers as Vance Packard. Here is the waste maker, the builder of status symbols, the clever manipulator of the masses, the creator of useless desires. Here—shrouded in mystery and dealing in the devil's own secrets—is a man endowed with powers that ordinary mortals do not possess. The most enlightened people in the world jump for him like puppets on a string, *for, according to this myth, he can sell anything to anybody.*

Since this myth can lead to costly errors, we must examine it. A complete description of it is available in any of dozens of recent books, articles, and columns; but we prefer the theories of John Kenneth Galbraith, as set down in his book, *The Affluent Society,* published by the Houghton Mifflin Company in 1958.

Here, if ever, is a singularly pure example.

The picture that Mr. Galbraith paints is frightening in its horror. Society is based on a thick substratum of cement heads who "do not . . . know what they want." The manufacturers, in turn, *produce what these people do not need.* Madison Avenue is then called on to work its wizardry; and the public, in a hypnotic state, marches off to buy billions of dollars worth of meretricious, gaudy, and useless products. Then the cycle repeats, a classic Greek drama where men go willy-nilly to their fate.

It is a picture of a paranoiac capitalism—a capitalism, as it were, gone mad. For most of these products, says Mr. Galbraith, fill no real need. They fill only an imaginary need. They are a useless, and senseless, outpouring:

> *"Since the demand would not exist if it were not contrived, its utility or urgency . . . is zero."*

What is the function of the advertising man in all this? Mr. Galbraith spells it out exactly:

> *"Their central function is to create desires—to bring into being wants that previously did not exist."*

"Desires," in other words, "are synthesized by advertising." This is "modern want creation." The public, like Pavlov's dog, will salivate on schedule when Madison Avenue rings the bell. Thus, everyone is caught up in a maelstrom of mustards and mattresses, "mauve and cerise, air-conditioned, power-steered, and power-braked automobiles," packaged foods, portable ice-boxes, cereals, detergents, and baby powders.

Mr. Galbraith mentions, for example, "a man who devised a nostrum for a non-existent need, and then successfully promotes both."

This interdependence between advertising and the producers, Mr. Galbraith calls "The Dependence Effect." Thus ". . . the production of goods creates the wants that the goods are presumed to satisfy." Once this premise has been set up, an entire corpus of subsequent ideas appears to be brilliantly illuminated.

To this role of advertising—creating wants "that previously did not exist"—Mr. Galbraith gives academic sanction of a sort. He writes:

"None of this is novel. All would be regarded as elementary by the most retarded student in the nation's most primitive school of business administration."

Perhaps.

However, it would have to be a most primitive business school, and the students would have to be most retarded and with a strong allergy for research as well, for none of this is remotely in accord with reality in advertising.

There is no such witchcraft in advertising. Advertising men have no such Svengali power. There is not, and has never been, "a man who devised a nostrum for a non-existent need, and then successfully promotes both." Advertising, in fact, has perhaps only *one* basic law. Countless agencies, thousands of manufacturers, and legions of bankrupts will take the stand and testify to its truth.

This law is:

IF THE

PRODUCT DOES NOT

MEET SOME EXISTING DESIRE

OR NEED OF THE CONSUMER,

THE ADVERTISING WILL

ULTIMATELY FAIL.

Mr. Galbraith has his facts exactly backwards.
Advertising does not synthesize desires.
Desires instead synthesize advertising.

The truth of this is not obvious at first glance; but bear with us, while we develop it, for it is of enormous importance to the manufacturer.

America, today, enjoys a profusion of products such as the world has never seen. Many of them are new, spectacular, dazzling, and ingenious. It is natural to assume that with them come new desires, new wants; and that these new products are, in essence, like toys to an insatiable and curious child. It is natural, too, to assume that the demand for them and the desire for them are whipped up by the vendor.

But there is a gap in this thinking. New forms of transportation do not create the *desire* for transportation. New forms of food do not create the *desire* for food. New forms of shelter do not create the *desire* for shelter. Do not confuse a *type* of shoe with the desire for shoes. Do not confuse a *method* of labor saving with the desire not to be a drudge. Do not confuse a *new kind* of illumination with the wish to banish the darkness.

Consider:

There is almost no kind of product now on the market that did not exist in more primitive form thousands of years ago. There are, of course, a few—but they represent a very thin frosting on our giant national economy.

Ancient Rome, for example, had perfumes, beds, rugs, mattresses, salves, pomades, pain remedies, mouthwashes, ointments, powders, soaps, stoves, clocks, jewels, rings, lip colorings, wines, beers, kitchen utensils, razors, cold storage, baths, oils, dentifrices, and hair creams—to mention only a few. Instead of the car, the ancient Roman had the chariot; instead of the engine, the horse; instead of electricity, the oil lamp; instead of the telegraph, the semaphore; instead of the press, the copyist; instead of the telephone, the messenger; instead of television, the entertainers; instead of the book, the scroll; instead of labor-saving devices, the back muscles of a slave.

But there was no *Via Madisonia.*

It is conceivable, actually, that an intelligent Roman, walking into our affluent society, might simply find himself in a better store.

What has happened—and what is happening—is a simple matter of product evolution. The industrial revolution, with its marvelous machines, has brought to the masses what used to be the possessions of a precious and privileged few, and the manufacturers, seeking serious gains, are engaged in making their products better and better. To assume that advertising is the *cause* is to state the case backwards. Advertising is only an *effect*—and the manufacturer who forgets this is out of touch, indeed, with reality.

Does a man need fire? Advertising has power only when it can offer him fire in an improved form—say, in a more modern stove. Does a man want transportation? Advertising has power only when it can offer him a better car. Does his head ache? Advertising has power only when it offers him remedies which can make his life more tolerable. Are his clothes dirty? Advertising has power only when it can show him easier, faster, and more civilized ways to wash. Do his wounds bleed? Advertising has power only when it can offer him better bandages. Does he shiver from cold? Advertising has power only when it can show him easier, cheaper, or more effective ways to stay warmer.

"Repeat purchases" are the economic scale on which these mass products are weighed, and the power of the advertising man is no greater than the power of his product to survive.

The phrase "product evolution" is not unapropos. The whole concept, in a way, is straight out of Darwin. There do appear, for a short while on the economic scene, wild mutations in products; they are senseless, and they are stupid; but such products are sooner or later doomed—like the pterodactyl, the brontosaurus, the archaeopteryx—to vanish into some economic Mesozoic shale.

The manufacturer who forgets this—and brings out foolish, frivolous, or unwanted products—is headed for extinction, for his competitors will not forget it.

At the very least, a manufacturer must match his competitors' products. If he is looking for real growth, he must excel them. John Crichton, the wise editor of *Advertising Age*, summed up this thesis recently in a very few words for a confused businessman. He said:

"If your Research and Development Department is only in the typewriter of some copy man, you are already lost."

We begin now to approach the true role of advertising in our economy. In the next chapter, we will examine it.

But first a word:

Are these products really needed? Are they a strict necessity? Mr. Galbraith may well have a point here, for the answer is "No." Pat Steel, at Young & Rubicam, put this argument as succinctly as it will ever be put:

"People don't really need these things.

"People don't really need art, music, literature, newspapers, historians, wheels, calendars, philosophy . . .

"All that people really need is a cave, a piece of meat, and possibly, a fire."

The New Entrepreneurs

Advertising is a $43,000,000,000 business. It has been growing, flourishing, and expanding for almost one hundred years. Yet a strange and startling fact exists: *There is no general economic theory on what advertising does and how it works.*

Economists handle advertising with suspicion; its critics give it credit for powers that it does not possess; its supporters defend it with all sorts of nonsense.

What *does* it do?

The secret of the Sphinx is that it has no secret. Perhaps the mystery of the advertising business is that it has no mystery. "If you go directly to the heart of a mystery," said Christopher Morley, "it ceases to be a mystery and becomes only a question of drainage."

Let us try, if we may, for some drainage.

Advertising is, actually, a simple phenomenon in terms of economics. *It is merely a substitute for a personal sales force*—an extension, if you will, of the merchant who cries aloud his wares. It puts rapidly in print (or on radio and television) what would otherwise have to be handled by word of mouth.

It does this at lower cost.

Advertising was born with the Industrial Revolution, when personal selling for mass goods became an impossibility; it grew with the Industrial Revolution, as improvements in technology spewed out still more goods; it became immense, as production became immense; *but it was always an effect—and never a cause.*

Advertising has no real magic that is not tied to the product itself. Thus in good times, when money is plentiful, it works magnificently; and in bad times, when money is scarce, it follows the sales of products down.

Advertising cannot combat a downtrend against a kind of product (witness buggy-whips, celluloid collars, and horses); and it cannot start an uptrend, as we have seen, unless there is some *a priori* utility or desire.

Martin Mayer, in *Madison Avenue, U.S.A.*, put it well:

"As on the political scene, advertising is wind on the surface, sweeping all before it when it blows with the tide but powerless to prevent a shifting of greater forces."

Can it be dispensed with?

We debated this question recently with a number of economists, and their conclusion was: "Yes." The reason they gave was an interesting one. They said:

"The only result would be a change in the time scale—the speed with which a new product would find its own level among the consumers."

This conclusion is interesting; but like many pure rationalizations—which are not empirical—it happens to be wrong. For there are many products that cannot demonstrate their own superiority to the consumer and, in today's economy, would never find their own level. They would, instead, die quietly on the economic vine.

Let us illustrate this with an imaginary case history:

The New Entrepreneurs
Without Advertising

*A young manufacturer devises a new breakfast
food with one half the calories, twice the essential vitamins, and twice the protein—with a
taste equal to that of his competitors.*

It sells at the same price.

*Simultaneously, his brother devises, by a new
process, a cigarette that removes 95% of the tars
from the smoke stream—yet is still rich to the
taste, delicious to smoke, and satisfying.*

Both of them, however, have products that are
not self-demonstrable to the public. They look,
taste, and seem the same as the old, rich, and
entrenched brands.

*There is no advertising, and there is no pos-
sibility of marketing either of these brands.*

*A $1,000,000 personal sales force at $2.00
a call (which is absurdly low) might be able to
tell a half-million people—just once!—about
these new brands.*

*As we have seen, this would result in no pen-
etration and would achieve nothing.*

Since the products are new, there is no demand.

*The giant chain stores, as well as the indepen-
dents—where every inch of shelf space is a price-
less commodity—say: "Without the demand, we
cannot spare you the room."*

*Another factor comes into play: Even if the
two new entrepreneurs could get distribution, it*

would not suffice. For a food will not keep indefinitely, and cigarettes stale rapidly. Fast turnover is essential to maintain product quality.

The products would die—depriving the economy of some of its competitive vitality.

Now let us examine the same case history in terms of what could happen in actual practice:

The Same Two New Entrepreneurs

Each manufacturer selects an introductory market. An advertising campaign, for the same $1,000,000, now buys 500,000,000 advertising impressions. The young entrepreneurs can now tell thirty, forty, or fifty million people—over and over again—the hidden advantages of these two products. The products may look the same, but people suddenly become aware that they are not the same.

Penetration soars.

Chains and independents are forced to accept distribution, for the consumer is the ultimate dictator of what goes on the retailers' shelves.

Sales begin to mount, for a previous desire exists, on the part of the public, for more healthful foods and less tars.

Profits mount.

Profits, in turn, are poured into more advertising and further expansion. Two aggressive new companies are added to the American economy; but something even more important happens.

The entrenched companies are forced to defend their own brands. As we have seen, this cannot be done with words. They must improve their products.
This they do, and counter-merchandising begins. Still better products emerge.

An excellent example of the truth of all this was seen recently in an action of the Federal Trade Commission. This government body coerced the tobacco industry into making no claims about low-tar cigarettes—regardless of whether or not these claims were true. This action came just as two dramatic new cigarettes were coming on the market, bringing the public the lowest tar ranges in history. These brands had cost millions of dollars to develop, but the manufacturers were thus unable to advertise their advantages. Overnight, they vanished from the retailers' shelves.

The phrase "new entrepreneurs," incidentally, applies not only to a new manufacturer, hopeful, wistful, and alone. It applies, equally, to mighty General Foods, seeking to introduce a new product against, say, mighty Standard Brands. For new products stand on their own feet in the marketplace, and the situation does not change.

It may seem, at first glance, of no consequence which firm has the business, but there is an enormous consequence. The producer, undisturbed by new competition, tends to monopolistic practices in form, quality, and price. The necessity for product improvement disappears. The new entrepreneurs vanish from the economic scene.

The ultimate of this principle is seen in the U.S.S.R. A recent cartoon in *Izvestia*, entitled "Twins Against Their Will," depicts a real-life situation in the Volga village of Sengilei. Here men, women, and children all wear identical checked hats, checked suits, and checked earmuffs—because these models are the only ones produced by a producer who lives in no fear of a competitive threat.

A casual reference to statistics shows the workings of this dynamic force in the economy. Over 60% of the products now on sale in supermarkets were not on sale fifteen years ago. $100,000,000 of the sales of Minnesota Mining & Manufacturing are in products unheard of six years ago. Over 70% of Procter & Gamble's sales are in products designed since 1946. Some 60% of Bristol-Myers' sales are from products introduced since 1949. Over half of Lever Brothers' sales come from products marketed since 1953.

Thus we arrive at the true role of advertising. It is not to create some "new desire," and fill it with some "useless product," for which the public has no "real need."

The true role of advertising is exactly that of the first salesman ever hired by the first manufacturer— to get business away from his competitors. Or, as the economists phrase it, to "shift the demand curve between products."

This is the restless American economy.

It is also economic liberty, and once economic liberty is abridged or destroyed, all other liberty is abridged or destroyed.

"Power over a man's subsistence," said Alexander Hamilton, "is power over his will."

36
A Call for Cannon Balls

In the sixteenth century, a young man named Galileo Galilei went up to the top of the leaning tower of Pisa and dropped two cannon balls. When they hit the earth, these cannon balls made an impact which will, without doubt, shape mankind's destiny to the last syllable of recorded time. For they put an end to a *method of thinking,* and the world can never be the same again.

The experiment was a simple one. It had been taught for 2,000 years that a heavy object fell faster than a light one. If it was twice as heavy, it fell twice as fast.

The authority? It was no less than the great Aristotle. He had said so, and for twenty centuries, like the processional caterpillars, mankind had accepted his dictum, blindly, as a fact. It came as a shock when Galileo dropped two balls—a heavy one and a light one—and the world witnessed that both hit the ground at the same time.

It was the beginning of the end of the Aristotelian, *prescientific* civilization, for, as Wendell Johnson points out:

> *"What Galileo demonstrated was not so much a fact about falling weights . . . as a new problem-solving method based not on the authority of age and prestige, but rather on the authority of observation and experiment."*

Hardly more than three hundred years have elapsed since Galileo; and after all, three hundred years is but a small part of the morning; yet in this time, the whole structure of civilization has changed.

For scientists began to perform experiments, to see *what* happened *when* something was done. It was refreshing, this new philosophy of "what-when." Many facts began to appear, suddenly, as fables. Wisdom and experience began to appear, often, as fallacies. Personal opinion began to appear as just that—personal opinion. How many a scientist, since Galileo, has watched an experiment with wide and wondering eyes, and said: "Things are not what they seem to be!"

It is time, now, that advertising men let fall some cannon balls. It is time, now, to find out not only what makes advertising more effective, but to accord advertising its rightful role in our economy and to put an end to the myths and distortions. For much of the battle between the slave world and the free world today is being fought out on economic grounds, on mankind's desire for a better life; and advertising is the voice of competition—the voice of free enterprise, in a free world.

It needs facts, not fables.

It needs principles and not opinions.

The issue, actually, is even wider than economics alone. For since Cain quarreled with Abel, the chasm between brothers has been their inability to talk to each other; and the principles hidden in advertising are fundamentally the principles of all communications.

Unfortunately, our advertising awards are still based on opinion, supposition, and aesthetics; we still spend much of our $43,000,000,000 a year on wishful thinking; and we have few men who will risk the loneliness of leaning towers. Advertising began as an art, and too many advertising men want it to remain that way—a never-never land where they can say: "This is right, because we *feel* it's right."

Earlier we told the story of the panel of top creative people from twenty-five big agencies who were asked to pick the three worst television commercials of the past several years; and how they picked (as the worst) two of the most electric successes of the past several decades. I spent several hours with one member of this panel, an agency president. Out of curiosity, I showed him Nielsen figures, penetration charts, market data, some rather revealing facts. He seemed to be in agreement until I mentioned the words "advertising laws."

"Laws!" he said. "The minute you introduce these, you destroy art, and advertising is an art."

Too many agency men—and clients, too—agree. They shy away from principles or any talk of advertising laws. They seem to think that principles restrict creative effort—rather than guiding it and making it richer and more profitable.

Such a viewpoint is, of course, the opposite of the scientific mind. Scientists believe only what they can weigh, measure, calculate, and observe. This is why scientists do not believe in ghosts. They seek out facts; they deduce principles; and then, within them, let their imaginations run riot.

In this way, scientists have remade the world.

Most advertising men, however, are still necromancers at heart. They do believe in ghosts. They listen to voodoo drums, whisper magic incantations, and mix, in their potions, eye of newt and ear of frog. Some day, like the barber surgeons of four hundred years ago, they must begin to look objectively at their craft. Somewhere, in our business, is the first true anatomist—a Vesalius, who will begin to trace the linkage of the tendons, or a Harvey, who will begin to speculate about the circulation of the blood.

Advertising will be on the way, then, to becoming a profession.

A Note about the Author

Rosser Reeves, *chairman of the board of Ted Bates & Company, is, at the age of fifty, a man with rather dazzling reserves of energy. His main preoccupation, of course, is one of the fastest-growing advertising agencies in America. However, in addition, he is a licensed pilot, a skilled yachtsman, a collector of modern art, a Civil War buff, a musician, and a writer of short stories; from time to time he immerses himself in chess, and as a nonplayer, he was captain of the last American chess team sent to Moscow. Born in Danville, Virginia, Mr. Reeves studied at the University of Virginia, and began his career as a reporter for the Richmond* Times-Dispatch. *But he soon gave up journalism in favor of advertising, coming to New York in 1934 and working for various agencies as a copywriter before joining Ted Bates and Company in 1940. He was vice-president and copy chief of the agency for six years, and became chairman of the board in 1955.* Reality in Advertising *is his first book.*

February 1961

A Note on the Type

The text of this book was set on the Linotype in a new face called PRIMER, *designed by* Rudolph Ruzicka, *earlier responsible for the design of Fairfield and Fairfield Medium, Linotype faces whose virtues have for some time now been accorded wide recognition. The complete range of sizes of Primer was first made available in 1954, although the pilot size of 12 point was ready as early as 1951. The design of the face makes general reference to Linotype Century (long a serviceable type, totally lacking in manner or frills of any kind) but brilliantly corrects the characterless quality of that face.*

Composed, printed, and bound by Kingsport Press, Inc., Kingsport, Tenn. Paper manufactured by S. D. Warren Co., Boston.

Typography and binding design by Herbert Bayer.